Liturgies in a Time When Cities Burn

Liturgies in a Time When Cities Burn

Keith Watkins

ABINGDON PRESS
Nashville & New York

SET UP, PRINTED, AND BOUND BY THE
PARTHENON PRESS, AT NASHVILLE,
TENNESSEE, UNITED STATES OF AMERICA

We live, today, in an anxious world. Later generations will probably see our age as a time of transition from one social order to another, as we find the Middle Ages a "middle" between the Graeco-Roman civilization and the full-fledged European. But we cannot see the present that way, because what we are moving toward does not yet exist, and we can have no picture of it. Nor is the ascendancy of Europe—the concert of nations consisting of white people, and their economic culture roughly coextensive with Christendom—as yet a finished act in history; but its form is broken. We feel ourselves swept along in a violent passage, from a world we cannot salvage to one we cannot see; and most people are afraid.

Susanne K. Langer in *Philosophical Sketches*

Preface

I speak to three accusers. A black barber in Seattle who, after church on the Sunday following Martin Luther King's burial, asked: "Now, professor, what can we do to keep people from smashing my windows still another time?" A white executive in Kansas City who asked: "Why are you so interested in changing around the order of worship? What difference does it make, anyway?" A bishop from New York state who asked me in correspondence: "Why don't seminary professors take sabbatical leaves with churches instead of universities? Have they lost their faith in the church?"

After six years of teaching at Christian Theological Seminary in Indianapolis, I moved my family to Seattle where I had been appointed Visiting Minister-Theologian at University Christian Church. For nine months I reported daily to an office in the church; I counseled with staff and passersby; I met with committees and boards, councils and classes; I preached and buried and presided in the liturgical assembly. Most of all I talked and listened. I tried to sense the mood of people in one large metropolitan congregation.

My sampling of opinion was more extensive than that afforded by this congregation, for I traveled widely, meeting church people in Yakima and Pendleton, Eugene and Portland, Oklahoma City and Stockton and Kansas City.

During this return to the church I also enjoyed academic privileges afforded by the University of Washington, and especially those of the Henry Suzzallo Library. My intention had been to read in anthropology and sociology in order to broaden my understanding of the cultural function of cultic acts. Quickly, however, my attention was diverted from reports of research to the generalizations made by philosophers who had studied primary data. Ernst Cassirer's extended analyses of how man can know captured my attention. Susanne K. Langer's expositions of the relation of cultural forms to human feeling shaped many of my reflections. Each of these gifted and productive scholars drew upon a wide range of scientific data, from both the exact and human sciences; each dealt with cultic acts with great perception and sensitivity. Although neither of them affirmed the Christian gospel as I do, each of them helped me understand my own experience more than has anyone since student days when Friedrich Schleiermacher's *Glaubenslehre* pointed me to a way of grasping the Christian faith with head as well as heart.

Although on leave from my regular duties, I continued certain professional responsibilities dealing with liturgical reform and Christian renewal and reunion. Wherever I went I talked with pastors and lay people about the principles that have arisen in this ecumenical age. I listened to their fears and tried to understand their impatience. Always I sought to stand on the far side of denominationalism and invited those whom I met to come along with me.

What I experienced and learned through the year, what I expounded to anyone who would listen and have written in the pages which follow, is briefly put. "In this time of violent passage various forms of the racial myth, with their intimations of the miraculous and the mysterious, have arisen to give us hope. The results—injustice, inhumanity, genocide, assassination —reveal the inadequacy of this way out of our deep anxiety. Impotent, too, is the traditional wisdom enshrined in the liturgies of the church, for Christian worship has been demonized, transmuted from a witness against us to a means of our self-justification. In order to lead us in creating a new society, in some time yet to come, the Christian liturgy of Word and Sacrament must be revivified, purged of its demonic traits, filled again with the qualities which it is supposed to have."

And while I did these things the cities burned.

Contents

Violent
Passage

The old order is passing away, that we know, dispatched in some cities by bombs and guns and in others by bulldozers and school buses and ballot boxes. As the exclusive covenants and tacit agreements that used to keep people in their places fall down, anxiety and defensiveness and aggressiveness rise up. Those of us who have enjoyed some of the good things of life—such as food and shelter and responsibility—sense that all this is threatened by the rising militancy of colored races, by the surge of industrial society, by the radical shifts in morality paraded by emancipated juniors. Little good it does to hear that rapid transit and automation mean a better life or that the new society will be richer and more satisfying than the old. What we fear is the loss of neighborhood and the displacement of ourselves long before the golden age is ushered in. We fight back as best we can, but so powerful are the forces driving our frail boats that we achieve no security, "swept along in a violent passage, from a world we cannot salvage to one we cannot see."

In his *Essay on Man,* written at the close of a career devoted to the study of man's spiritual-intellectual work, Ernst Cassirer suggests a way of interpreting the anxiety of people today. He speaks of a "tension between stabilization and evolution," between one tendency "which seeks to preserve old forms" and another which "strives to produce new ones." This "ceaseless struggle between tradition and innovation, between reproductive and creative forces," is raging today.

In our time the innovative forces are the stronger; they verge on revolution, on the overthrow of everything that has been before. The most powerful of these driving energies is the scientific civilization that has already conquered the world. My mother was born on the day that the Wright brothers flew off of Kitty Hawk, and now I cross the continent

14

with scarcely time to eat a good lunch. Vast changes of this order would be convulsive enough if they affected only those of us prepared for such a time by a thousand years of cultural history. Yet the most primitive tribes of man are now coming into this same world—and with the forces of politics being what they are, some of these men one generation out of the bush and animism are closer to controlling scientific civilization than are most of us whose culture has been maturing since the time of Plato.

Scientific civilization is a monster with three heads: the military, the industrial establishment, and the university. These three institutions are the "somebodies" whom governments of our time are trying to satisfy. Their wants determine how things are going to be. Scientific civilization feeds on the bodies of young men and women and children killed in war. Planned obsolescence is one of its products. The crowding of our cities and the polluting of waterways and atmosphere come from it, as does the immediacy of communication—which helps us know one another better but which also intensifies tension and revolution. But what catches everyone of us is the sense of being rushed faster than we can go. We are like little children being jerked along so quickly that our feet vibrate over the pavement instead of running over it. We have, says Archibald MacLeish, the "sense that we are getting nowhere far too fast and that, if something doesn't happen soon, we may arrive."

The forces of revolutionary change surge forward, which is enough to cause our alarm, but at the very same time the forces that conserve the past are losing strength. Chief among these conserving forces is traditional wisdom—an unexamined and unquestioned view of the meaning of life, a cosmic understanding expressed in religious rite and dogma. In our time this link with the past is weakening. In a strange travelogue, *Their Heads Are Green and Their Hands Are Blue,* Paul Bowles illustrates this decline of cosmic wisdom in non-Christian portions of the world. One episode was a journey that he made from Morocco, before any serious attempts to modernize that country had been undertaken, to Turkey, which was already deeply involved in the process. Both countries were Moslem; but in Morocco the ancient piety and way of life were still functioning, while in Turkey the effort to bring the nation into the twentieth century had caused the breakdown of many old ways. Against better advice, Bowles took with him his Moroccan servant Abdeslam. This orthodox Moslem was scandalized by what he found in Turkey, for his good and happy world, assailed from all sides, was crumbling before his eyes. He could not have understood, says Bowles, "if I had explained to him that what he calls religion the modern world calls superstition." And then Bowles speaks about all of us as much as about Abdeslam: "Something will have to be found to replace the basic wisdom which has been destroyed, but the discovery will not be soon; neither Abdeslam nor I will ever know of it."

A similar decline in the strength of traditional wisdom is portrayed in Jessamyn West's novel *A Matter of Time*. In a California home two middle-aged sisters spend a summer waiting for one of them to die of cancer. During the weeks of waiting they reconstruct their lives, remembering all that had passed between them during the years since the one first held her infant sister in her arms. In all these experiences now relived there is no religion, for the family's "Pilgrim faith" had disappeared in their grandmother's generation, leaving only the shell of what had once been their people's basic wisdom. At bedtime these two women do have a ritual of sorts—a rythmic stroking of fragrant grease into their faces as their mother and grandmother before them had done. At bedtime they were bound to the past "not by memories of prayers said or Bible stories read" but by "memories of devotions of another kind. Face creams hold the generations together."

Church-going is still widespread among us, and it will continue to be; yet its claim upon our time and life has weakened. We continue to affirm the doctrines and principles of an earlier generation, but we

17

pick our words more carefully now lest we say more than we are willing to say. There is a readiness not present two decades ago to receive *Honest to God* and *The Secular City* and *Situation Ethics*. People still engage in religious practices, yet their performance is not quite convincing.

In this kind of intellectual climate myths are likely to grow. Driven by our fears we pluck the fruit from these new growths; we and our life together are transformed into a new configuration.

Once before, when man lived in this kind of violent passage, the new myths dealt with the cities of man and of God. The epic stories that had expressed the traditional wisdom of Greece and Rome no longer satisfied, and in their place grew new myths of creation and covenant and crucifixion. Jesus of Nazareth was the central figure, and the faith inspired by him captured the world. A bishop of the church, facing the destruction of the classical culture, praying that the city might be preserved, created the new forms of thought that enabled people swept along in that violent passage to reach the far shore safely. The culture of the West since Augustine's time fourteen centuries ago is convincing proof that the myths that grew then were wholesome.

The firstfruits of myths to grow in our time of violent passage, however, are bitter indeed. During World War II occupation forces executed some two hundred thousand Russian Jews. Fifty thousand were massacred at a place called Babi Yar, near Kiev. After brooding over this event for twenty years Anatoly Kuzmetsov, who was a twelve-year-old boy when the slaughter took place, wrote a book about the event. Late in the story he comments that he wrote about nothing exceptional, "but only about ordinary things that were part of a *system:* things that happened just yesterday, historically speaking, when people were exactly as they are today." A long period of preparation readied the soil for the savagery that came into flower in mid-twentieth century Western culture. In his *Myth of the State* Cassirer traces its recent history to Thomas Carlyle, who developed a reasoned exposition of a theory of hero worship. As he spoke to London audiences, Carlyle intended no revolution but instead wished to "stabilize the social and political order" and believed that the veneration of moral exemplars was the way to do it. Arthur Gobineau blended this kind of hero worship with race worship, asserting in his writings that all forces in the life of man are underlings to race, which is "the *only* master and ruler of the historical world." Hegel next worked the soil. In his maturity he combined a system of ethics and a philosophy of right into a "ruthless imperialistic nationalism." He was convinced that in every age the "world spirit" becomes incarnated in one nation to which all others must be subordinated.

The intellectual soil ready, all that is needed is the right weather and someone to sow the seed of new myths. The climate comes: a critical moment in man's social life, a time of unusual and dangerous happenings, a period when the old structures are falling away and the new ones are not yet built, a time of violent passage when we are torn loose from our anchor and driven down a gorge toward a future we cannot yet see. "In desperate situations man will always have recourse to desperate means," says Cassirer. "If reason has failed us, there remains always the *ultima ratio,* the power of the miraculous and mysterious."

When that weather is right, a political leader sows the seed of myth. He devises a new explanation of the meaning of things and casts it in the imaginative and potent language of epic story. The climate was right in Germany in the period after the first World War, and Adolf Hitler sowed the seed. By 1933 the political world was alarmed at Germany's rearmament, but already the mental rearmament had taken place. The political myth of the superrace destined to rule the world had already been created and accepted.

A sustained case study of the twisted moral power that so nearly destroyed Western culture is Langdon Gilkey's *Shantung Compound,* a fully documented and interpreted accounting of his prison experiences during that same war. Fifteen hundred Europeans and Americans in north China were crowded into a tiny mission compound by Japanese occupation forces. At Christmastime, after they had suffered two years of near starvation and extreme anguish together, they received a shipment of food parcels from the American Red Cross. There were enough for one apiece if divided among the entire population of the prison, eight apiece if divided among the Americans only. At this point the community of suffering nearly broke apart, for the majority of the Americans were adamant in their insistence that the American goods should go to Americans only. Had it not been for the Japanese guards patrolling the compound, Gilkey comments, civil strife might have broken out among the prisoners.

What is so astonishing about this incident is the way in which distorted national pride asserted itself. For two years these former strangers had been bound together in a life that erased their differences. In all the struggles for survival they had shared with one another. But now, unexpectedly, this new element changed the circumstances, and a twisted form of patriotism appeared. There was no Hitler in that prison to sow the seed of the racial myth. There did not have to be, for, like the seeds of dandelions and crabgrass, the seeds of racial myths are in the air and in the ground, needing only favorable conditions in which to sprout.

Gilkey's later reflections call attention to the fact that men generally act in an immoral fashion when their interests are at stake. Yet, they remain moral enough "to wish to *seem* good" even if they cannot possibly be good. Rarely does self-interest come nakedly into the open as the selfishness that it is. More often "a legal, moral, or even religious argument" is advanced to defend selfish actions.

Kuzmetsov and Cassirer and Gilkey are describing the same phenomenon, the coming together of three conditions: (1) *a time of crisis or desperation that* (2) *threatens our most important personal needs, and* (3) *results in recourse to desperate means by which to preserve and advance those needs.* In our century the miraculous and mysterious is the racial myth. For Germans earlier in this century, the myth took the form of the superrace. For Americans in prison during the war with Japan it was American stuff for Americans only. In the cities of our nation now it is the rising form of black power. In the suburbs and countryside it is the lingering conviction of white supremacy.

What of the acts of worship still performed in this time of violent passage? What of the stylized corporate ritual that we conduct ceaselessly in our churches? It has become a form of our self-deception, a mask that conceals our pride of race and position, the source of new ways of justifying devotion to our own security. It is bad enough when our churches espouse, in the name of God, causes and principles that are wrong—property over persons, privilege over sacrifice, the established order over justice, the city of man over the city of God. It is even worse when this is done so as to confirm us in the most destructive of all human traits of character. No wonder that some branches of new theology are increasingly popular. Once pride was the prime sin; now it is sloth. Self-esteem has become a virtue and the acceptance of responsibility the goal toward which men should be encouraged. But, says Kenneth Hamilton, this point of view which seems so modern is a traditional one harking back to the brave new world of the enlightenment. This "wanting too much to excel," so valued by the enlightenment and contemporary thought, is the older tradition's definition of sin.

Yet, this kind of gospel combining self-esteem and the duty of being as industrious as possible resounds from our pulpits and speaks quietly in prayers. It pervades church life and contributes a major ingredient to the inability of churches to affect the character of life and of the institutions of contemporary society. For when we spend our time reinforcing our self-esteem and encouraging ourselves to continue what we are doing, but with greater zeal, we are using religion with its power to perpetuate those very traits which religion is supposed to witness against. Charles Y. Glock and Rodney Stark recently published an important study of the ways in which the teachings of the churches have shaped American attitudes toward Jews. Their findings indicate that approximately 17.5 million Americans "hold fairly strong anti-Semitic beliefs" and at the same time rank high in an index of religious bigotry. One researcher is a Christian; one is not. "But as the findings were revealed," they said, "both of us shared equally a sense of shock and dismay that a faith which proclaims the brotherhood of man can be so perverted into a *raison d'etre* for bigotry." The churches are implicated in the crisis of black and white in our land. The Klan has its Kludd, the patriotic organization its chaplain, the white establishment its Protestant preacher. By our silence we have condoned, by our ignorance we have perpetuated, by our failure to act we have deepened the inhuman conditions of life; by explicit teaching we have fostered the prejudice that threatens now to destroy our nation.

What Gerhard von Rad says of Cain and his sin is true for us. Its terribleness is that it catches us not at

24

the point where we forget ourselves in human life, but precisely at the point where we lift our hands to God, at the altar. More clearly now than at any time in a century we can hear the prophet Isaiah:

> Your country lies desolate,
> your cities are burned with fire;
> in your very presence
> aliens devour your land;
> it is desolate, as overthrown by aliens.
> And the daughter of Zion is left
> like a booth in a vineyard,
> like a lodge in a cucumber field,
> like a besieged city. (Isaiah 1:7, 8)

From the grief of the crisis in our land we know that the prophet's threat has come true for us:

> When you spread forth your hands,
> I will hide my eyes from you;
> even though you make many prayers,
> I will not listen. (Isaiah 1:15)

There are times when I feel like stopping at this point. So often our rites are connected with the real life that should be destroyed rather than with the real life that God desires for mankind. There is another possibility. Instead of intensifying our problems and justifying our selfish course of action, Christian worship is still capable of steadying us in this time of violent passage. It can help us root out the poisonous racial myths and provide the seeds for new and life-giving myths that will sustain us in the time to come.

Ritual Becoming High Art

I still hear reports of growing church membership, of increasing attendance, of the continued expansion of the religious institution. I hear more often the despairing admission that everything is slacking off, no matter how hard one works, regardless of the imaginativeness of program undertaken. Most disconcerting of all is the evidence that those who find it hardest to take part in the church's liturgical life are the younger members of our society.

Yet this recognition of the weakness of current

forms cannot be interpreted to mean that highly
stylized, ritual behavior will cease. Some may drop
the stylized forms of the church, but they cast about
for new ones to take their place. The hunger for
ritual partially explains the urgency of musical genres
which have become so important during the past
decade. They are searchings for a new liturgy, new
ways of asking questions about the meaning of life,
new ways of stating a basic wisdom that can support
a person through this pilgrimage. While some of the
music is gay and playful, much of it, to use words
suggested by Peter Schrag, "is no brighter than a
silver cloud with a dark lining." This new folk music
connects the generations, but by means of a coherent
and "highly ironic declaration of disaffection." Home
life is stereotyped as the kind with money and no
love that drives children away. Emptiness and despair
and failure, which everyone knows are part of life, are
the heritage from the past remembered and thus con-
served for those now growing up. The result is bound
to be an intensification of the disaffection. Jim Morrison, spokesman for a musical group called The
Doors, states this mood well: "I'm interested in everything about revolt, disorder, chaos, especially activity
that has no meaning. It seems to me to be the road to
freedom." Of Los Angeles he says: "This city is
looking for a ritual to join its fragments." That ritual,

"a sort of electric wedding," is what The Doors have tried to provide.

When described in this way contemporary folk culture becomes a highly secularized and disciplined rehearsal of right attitudes. It is a slow dance that conserves one view of life and preserves the living center of a powerful social world. The vitality of this folk music of our time is an indication that the forces that preserve continuity and tie us to the past continue to operate even in a time when the forces to innovate are clearly the more powerful and effective. But we know when we listen to the melancholy remembrances that our hold on the past is tenuous at best.

And the world that is to come? Pop music promises the illusion of "Lucy in the sky with diamonds," of rides in a "boat on a river with tangerine trees and marmalade skies." But we want to keep more of the past and have more substantial visions of the future. The problem is how.

The answer that I want to give is the renewal of the Christian liturgy and the revivification of the basic wisdom that it expresses and communicates to the generations still to come. For this renewal to happen Christian worship must be purged of its demonic traits and filled again with the qualities that it is supposed to have. Two lines of thought support my answer: a particular understanding of the nature of liturgical rites and their function in human culture, and a specific view of the tragic character of the Christian vision of life's meaning.

To understand the cultural function of worship in our time we must trace the rise of symbolic forms, the intellectual-spiritual acts that human beings devise in response to the world they experience. The beginning point of human knowledge—of the world and of oneself—is the moment when the blur of colors and movements and sounds is stopped. Some object, some sound, something that passes by is seized by the mind and concentrated upon. It takes on a shape that can be remembered, reflected upon, compared with other impressions. In its simplest state, says Cassirer, this fixing of experiences into shapes is two-faced. The world sometimes suggests lifeless things; it sometimes gives the impression of life or potency. Thinglike and person-like are the two styles in which the world presents itself. But we are never satisfied with these unformed impressions. The mind works, driving toward understanding, and this it achieves by creating symbolic forms. Science and language, art and myth, are the results when a human mind spontaneously creates an enduring form that gathers up what had been experienced in formless and meaningless fashion. Although the symbolic form is necessarily removed from the immediacy of the experience, it is man's most valuable asset, the key to his humanity, the instrument by which he knows what the world is, what he himself is, and how he can gain mastery over all that is.

Cassirer states that the sciences like physics are the final development of the thinglike world that is part of the earliest and least formulated of our human experiences. But there is another side to the development of the human intellectual-spiritual life. Growing out of the unformed experience of the person-like world are the symbolic forms of art and religion. This side of cultural life begins with the perception of person or potency in the passing stream of phenomena. In the earliest stage of abstraction this power is identified with certain natural objects, like rocks, and with people. Gradually, the human spirit drives toward greater abstraction of this experience in the cultural or symbolic forms of religion. Very early in the process of objectification two streams develop—ritual and myth. Ritual begins when the mystery of life seems to focus in and around specific objects. Awestruck by such manifestations of potency, people respond with the actions that they believe to be demanded by the divinity whom they there encounter. From that time on, sight of the object recalls to mind the awesome presence and demands from them the disciplined rehearsal of right attitudes. This disciplined rehearsal is the beginning of worship. It may be crude or highly developed, depending in part on the character of the personified potency, depending in part on the general cultural level of the worshipers.

In the early history of a society this rehearsal takes the form of dance and is probably the earliest type of culture. It requires a group of people and it calls into play the simplest types of art—the movement of the body in rhythmic and coordinated patterns. Through the generations perceptions of mystery and theological interpretations of experience become more sophisticated. People move beyond the crudity of primitive understandings, replacing them with intellectual formulations that account more precisely for all that takes place. And the disciplined rehearsal of right attitudes changes too. Primitive communal dance becomes the complex version of Byzantine court ceremonies that we now know as the Divine Liturgy celebrated in Orthodox Churches. Even our relatively informal free churches manifest this ordered precision of the slow dance, of the disciplined rehearsal of right attitudes before something that represents divine mystery. Watch the deacons some Sunday when they collect the offering and distribute the communion. Note how people sit in the same pew Sunday by Sunday. Listen for the recurrent phrasing in prayers. Reflect upon the connection between what we do in church in highly stylized fashion and what we believe to be true, and what it demands of us.

Myth begins when the world at large, the nation or the tribe, the family or the individual, are experienced as centers of power. The organizing capacity of the human spirit seeks to relate these powers into a pattern. This process may be characterized by wishful thinking, in which case the product is a fantasy story or folktale in which a cultural hero acts in heroic proportions. When the more profound characteristic of moral orientation is dominant, the result is cosmic myth or metaphor in which the gods participate. In the myth the centers of power are articulated, organized in some scheme, arranged in a hierarchy of importance or power.

Ritual and cosmic myth are closely related. Each in its own way becomes what Langer calls a life symbol, an objectification of moral orientation, of cosmic relationship, of personal identity. Myth and ritual can function as life symbol because they are taken seriously; they carry with them the force of truth. Power is experienced in the presence of the sacred object; the interpretation commands acceptance because it, better than any other method of interpretation, expresses the meaning perceived in experience. Both lines of development carry ethical implications, for style of life is quickly encompassed as an extension of the disciplined rehearsal before the sacred object and as the expression of moral orientation objectified in myth.

Myth and ritual are well advanced stages in the gradually developed process of perceiving the world as person-like thing. There is, however, a further stage, the one reached when cosmic myth is finally cast as epic poetry. Bound together in the one literary element are two factors: an explanation of the nature and meaning of things, and purified forms of emotional response.

Even this stage is surpassed in the gradual formation of symbolic forms. There comes a time when the two factors bound together in cosmic myth are separated—emotion and rational meaning are factored out so that each stands by itself. One of the elements that results is philosophy, the "rationalization of vision," the casting in logical and reasoned speech of the perception of meaning that previously had been expressed in imaginative story. The other element is art, "the envisagement of feeling." In enduring form that can be seen or felt or heard, the feeling that had been associated with cosmic myth now stands clear.

What has finally come into being, although we have left out some of the steps, is a threefold pattern of human action: discursive thought that states in precise, logical form the factual nature of things; art that expresses the "felt life," or subjectivity, the "big unfolding of feeling in the organic, personal pattern of a human life, rising, growing, accomplishing destiny and meeting doom"; and personal action or ethical behavior. These three are so tied together that each informs and chastens the other. Although the cultural form has changed during this process, developing from slow dance to high art, it still expresses human response to the person-like quality that we encounter in our experience with the world around.

Where does worship, as conducted by a mature religion, fit in this scheme? It is the synthesis of ritual and cosmic myth, a part of the middle range in the long process by which man moves from the simplest types of experience to the creation of highly abstract symbolic forms. Worship is pre-philosophy/pre-art. It is life symbol not yet fully rationalized, not yet factored into discursive thought and artistic expressions of the felt life.

So long as Greek religion, philosophy, and art are illustrations used in expounding this model of human symbolization, we have little problem. We can see, with no sense of personal threat, that the time comes when their ritual and cosmic myth no longer are taken with complete seriousness, when what remains are philosophy and art. To use our own religious and cultural tradition as the source of illustrations is more difficult. Even here, however, we find evidence of this pattern of development. It is a cliché too little examined that the Hebrew religious mind was historically oriented. God was perceived in historical events. But what do we do with the tradition that Yahweh was first a storm deity, a variation of the holy object—in this case thunderbolts and lightning flashes?

> The voice of the Lord makes the oaks to whirl,
> and strips the forests bare;
> and in his temple all cry, "Glory!"
>
> (Psalm 29:9)

The exodus from Egypt fits our notion of the spiritualized nature of Hebrew religion, for again it seizes upon an actual event in history as the incarnation of potency. Yet in the Old Testament narratives the personification of potency that commanded contemplation and gave rise to disciplined rehearsal of right attitudes was a smoking mountain in the wilderness of Sinai. Most Christians today have moved far from this stage of the development of the Hebraic religious consciousness. Their vision has been partially rationalized, for they know what causes thunderstorms.

The change to high art has come to Christian ritual and myth just as it has for Greek. The Homeric epics took Greek religion to the highest level of cultural development that it could reach. Even when people found more rationalized ways of affirming what had once been affirmed by myth, the Homeric epics survived as high art. In our time as well as then these epics create for the reader an aesthetic experience—the illusion of human life set in the cosmic order with fate and fortune, history and destiny properly accounted for and organized. But we know this fleeting experience to be an illusion. For us it is not the strongest statement of which we are capable concerning the nature of life and reality. However true the epic may be in revealing human emotion, there is factual discrepancy, and in that sense it lacks truth. Just as we read Homer, so many in our time read the Gospel of Luke or listen to the religious compositions of Bach or Vaughan Williams. For them the ritual and myth of the Christian religion are high art, true to human experience, but not factual truth that fully commands their intellectual loyalty.

So long as we restrict ourselves to description of cultural forms, refusing to prescribe what ought to be, there is no escaping the conclusion that Christian worship in our time is *cosmic myth becoming philosophy/ritual becoming high art.* The participial form of this statement is important, for this grammatical device indicates a process now underway. Christianity, as a vital and vigorous force, exists today both as *ritual/cosmic myth* and as *high art/philosophy.* Christians, both ordinary believers and academic theologians, engage in the intellectual process that we have called the rationalization of vision and the artistic process that we have called the envisagement of feeling. Other Christians, both ordinary believers and academic theologians, affirm the compelling power of cosmic myth.

In both stages of cultural development the stories they tell are the same. Beginning with the creation of the cosmos by the power of God, the narrative turns to the calling of a particular nation to embody God's purposes. Men like Abraham and Moses, David and Isaiah, command the attention of everyone who reads these stories. Obviously human like the rest of us, these heroic figures nevertheless proclaim visions of truth that come from God himself. In this line of great men, but mysteriously superior to all of them, is Jesus of Nazareth. This carpenter's son secured the marveling support of the poor people of his land. There was no philosophical discussion of political theory, no use of military force to inflict fear on the people, no ordinary demogoguery. Yet his personal presence, his overwhelming sense of immediacy, his utter lack of pretension, combined to capture the loyalty of the people. There was more to him than personal presence. People sensed in him the same cosmic power that Moses had encountered in the burning bush, that led Abraham to a far country, that Jacob met while sleeping on a rock in the wilderness dreaming of a golden staircase going into heaven. Jesus drove people out of the temple, with eyes flashing, and the common people experienced cosmic power.

It may be beside the point to discuss whether the Christian liturgy in our time is viewed as cosmic myth or high art. Cosmic myth is an assertion of truth expressed in imaginative form and with deep feeling. It is convinced that this imaginative form is factually true and that it expresses values that compel acceptance. High art is an imaginative form that expresses deep feeling and moral value. But this expression is only slightly concerned with factual truth, with the data that can be measured scientifically. The claims for truth that high art makes are lighter than those that cosmic myth makes.

In either case, whether the imaginative form be accepted as cosmic myth or high art, it has compelling power; in either case it serves as a symbol of social reality. In every community, every social reality, there is something that provides the unifying center and invigorating heartbeat. Something matters more than anything else and therefore shapes everything that people think and do. Although this center of cultural life may not be clearly realized, it does take form in doctrines and unquestioned assumptions, in social institutions and customs. When faced with these manifestations of the most important, people respond with a disciplined rehearsal of right attitudes, with a slow dance, with worship. Generation by generation the vision of reality is preserved by the slow dance, and the community which depends upon that vision continues to live. Children encounter this vision when they are brought to the slow dance. Even before they can think, they understand. They become part of the people who know that life is this way rather than some other way.

We now can ask what vision Christian worship embodies. Whether it is considered to be cosmic myth or high art, what view of life does this stylized form convey? To what kind of future society does it lead? One way of answering these questions is by way of an analysis of a current conflict in literature. Many people today see a vision of man "in which madness and emotional degradation and illicit 'love' and drug addiction are more true than sanity and emotional harmony and health and love itself." Writers in this vein, says Archibald MacLeish, are raising a question not about a new chapter in the history of man but about the end of the book. They are challenging the understanding of what the life of man is about—an understanding that has been dominant in the West since the days of Greece, that supports the civilization of Europe and America. In the writings of men like Paul Bowles characters "robbed of purpose, their spirits rubbed flat, move zombielike through exquisitely desolate landscapes. . . . Displaced in the present, they have vague pasts and menacing futures; sighing despair, they search for something unnameable." MacLeish, and writers like him, choose not to agree with the authors of this new literature of extreme situations. He still believes in man as the wonder of the world because man is still its master. Even though man knows that he will die, he still creates and builds, tames beasts and builds cities.

This vision of man's nature, this understanding inherited from our fathers, is the kind of social reality that the Christian faith embodies and communicates. As Christians we must take the matter a further step, for our understanding of man is sharpened by the representative man, Jesus of Nazareth. Unfortunately, the way we have depicted him obscures his representative character. He has been made, says Donald Atwell Zoll, into "an apparently ineffectual and ascetic Nordic in a vague Levantine costume, feeding a group of sheep of obviously Anglo-Saxon breeding, seemingly in a sort of Rousseau-like revery, considering what new boons to offer humanity." This fictitious depiction will no longer do.

Are there ways of portraying that man that do speak to our age? There is hope that the answer is positive in some of the paintings produced by artists of our time. Phillip Evergood's "The New Lazarus" is an example. It portrays the evils of our time—a lynched Negro, a dead soldier, a flayed lamb, and

41

the crucified Christ. In the background are examples of the indifferent ones—a self-indulgent woman who refuses to look, a clown who refuses to listen, a pious churchman who refuses to speak. The picture is ugly, but the events it portrays are ugly, too. It is an event from the past of long ago, but it belongs to our time as well. Hans Hofmann's "Easter" is a swirl of orange and yellow, with heavy lines of black suggesting shapes of buildings and movements. The blackness depicts the world in which we live where the passions and prejudices, the hungers for power and wealth, drive men toward violence and cruelty. But Easter is the assertion of God's victory. In his picture Hofmann has painted a frail, fernlike spiral that springs forth from the blackest part of the picture. It moves upward with the impression of power that will be able to overcome even the blackest night of this world. This faith is what sustains Christians through all the struggles in this world.

What is important about these paintings is that they come from the modern world, depicting with the stuff of our time the representative stories of Jesus of Nazareth that are the foundation of our faith. Christ's passion and victory are thus revivified, brought into our time, so that their timelessness is evident to all men. The many episodes in which he figures, the many teachings that he delivers, are all of a kind:

"He who finds his life will lose it, and he who
loses his life for my sake will find it."

(Matt. 10:39)

It is the conviction that pain, frustration, loss,
tragedy are not in vain; that life is larger than any
one of us and that, therefore, it warrants every sacrifice that we can pay: It is is the conviction, to
borrow words from Alfred North Whitehead, "that
high aims are worthwhile" so that men may "wander
beyond the safe provision of personal gratifications."

A long time has gone by since Jesus lived among
men, demonstrating this vision of reality. Since then
many potent men have entered into history bearing
their own embodiments of meaning and power. In
our generation, too, there have been such people who
command the allegiance of the populace not so much
by what they say as by the mystique that surrounds
them wherever they go. We meet them face to face
on TV screens, in the newspapers, and in the streets.
In contrast we know Jesus only second hand, reading
the cold lines of type in books, hearing sacred music
inspired by him, celebrating the sacrament of bread
broken in his memory. Yet that power still comes
through, and we, too, walk on the edge of the crowd
who jostled to see him and to hear the tone of his
voice. At Christmastime we do. The talk of babies
and shepherds and mangers is but thin camouflage to

43

the mysterious man of long ago whose eyes capture ours and command our loyalty. And during Holy Week we sense his powerful presence—in the solemn and foreboding journey that led from the grandeur of Palm Sunday to the abasement of Good Friday. Whatever our personal faith, whatever our own style of life, we cannot but be moved by this "strange Jew, humorless and fanatic," who died alone rather than turn back from the way that was right for him, who experienced as profound a sense of estrangement as our race knows and yet remained true to his inner purposes, who by the unyielding consistency of his own life demonstrated how God's purposes continue unbroken despite all the crises of the earth's history.

Yet we experience a rising sense of exultation. This is because Jesus' death is an example of great tragedy rather than annihilation. Bound together in his passion are disaster and triumph, earthly pessimism and the "conviction of human worth and the divine splendour of things." His violent and wasteful death, in the words of Charles G. Bell, is consumed in a "flame of tacit and spiritual victory." When we look carefully we see ourselves in that man. We are caught in the prisons of our own lives, suffering because of family crisis, because of the threat of death in battle, because of dreams disappointed by life that is too far gone. We, too, cry out to God and no answer comes. Yet we sense that our lives, like his, need not be crushed by the powers of this world that tower over us. Though we do not see God with our own eyes, we do see the man of sorrows whose death has brought new life to so many people. And we can see ourselves as tragic figures too. We pay the price of life—sacrificing ourselves for our children, working for ideals greater than our own private interests, facing death for causes in which we believe. Seeing him we can believe that such is the way of the universe; we can face crises in personal life and nation, confident that, like him, we too will experience the consumption of our tragedies in a "flame of spiritual victory."

Feeling
and Form

Worship is a symbolic form that combines words and actions in a stylized expression of the experience of ultimate concern. When purged of its demonic traits Christian worship embodies a tragic vision of life, including anguish and victory, and incorporates people into a community whose common life manifests this sacrificial quality. In this time of violent passage we must give ourselves to this renewal of authentic liturgical form and revivification of the faith that it incarnates. Yet efforts to do so are frequently hampered by conflicting loyalties to feeling and form, to immediacy of experience and authoritative standards governing form. Before turning to a consideration of liturgical style and form for our time, I want to suggest a way through this conflict of loyalties.

From St. Louis to Seattle, while enjoying our airlines luncheon, an Episcopal layman and I debated liturgical reform. He was unhappy with the efforts of his church to revise their liturgy and to use contemporary forms of English. The world is changing rapidly, he said, and there must be some things that do not change. For him, the archaic English of his prayers is one of these changeless commodities. If he were Roman Catholic, he said, he would fight to keep the Mass in Latin; if he were Orthodox he would vote for Old Slavonic in church instead of new English.

We must take this point of view seriously, for liturgy, in contrast to preaching, does connect us with the church of all the ages. It is necessary to retain the form of words and intellectual structures that are found in the Bible and that shape our ways of worship because that form is so closely tied to the Christian view of reality. This vision, as Whitehead says, had three phases in its formation, the first and last primarily intellectual and the middle one moral. The first phase was accomplished by Plato, who near the end of his career concluded that the divine ele-

47

ment in the world accomplishes its purposes by persuasion rather than by force. The second phase was carried out by Jesus, who revealed this persuading God in the guise of mother and child, in the person of a homeless and lowly man, in the example of a tragic life lived in an aura of victory. The third phase was carried out by the theologians in the first Christian centuries who systematized the intuition that Plato had asserted and Jesus had infused with driving moral force.

This whole view of the meaning of things shaped the biblical culture and the classical style of Christian worship. Into this world of thought and moral power we enter when we participate in traditional Christian worship. Professors and pastors hesitate to depart from biblical language and traditional forms in the fear that by doing so they would lose hold of the reality that these forms preserve. If a group of professors is asked to revise our ways of worship, they begin with the tradition—New Testament, early Christian, Reformation. In time they get around to assessing the mood of moderns. As a result, a service that they prepare, such as the order that has been developed by the Commission on Worship of the Consultation on Church Union, is definitely conservative. Their rendering of the Lord's Prayer may bring quite a shock to people who have said the prayer in the older styles, but it is nothing when compared with

Malcolm Boyd's "Are you running with me, Jesus?"

There is another side to the matter. Ask a group of teen-agers what they think about the Sunday service of worship, and they are likely to complain about its formality, its stiffness, its inflexibility, its lack of beat. They want something to happen. The old words, the outdated music, the ceremonies with bread and wine, the whole archaic mess, is what they reject. They want readings from the newspapers to replace those from the Scriptures and lyrics by Bob Dylan to replace those by Charles Wesley. Worship, if it is to be at all, is to be relevant and contemporary, and, to use the word of one teen-ager, bubbly.

We dare not speak too harshly of these iconoclasts, for they learned their attitudes from their elders. Most of us have long evaluated church life by means of its effect upon our own emotional nature. Preaching is good if it stirs us, music is good if it moves us, ceremonies are good if they inspire us, worship is good if it enriches us. When these qualities are present we go, and when they are absent so are we. Youth have learned the same approach, and herein is the problem. What turns us on often turns them off. On a Sunday when one university student says that for one hour the church was in the twentieth century, a grandfather leaves the place of worship with clenched fists.

What we have to contend with is a struggle between feeling and form, between personal taste and external standards. Form enables worship to serve as a symbol of social reality; feeling enables a person to appropriate that reality. When they conflict, as they so often seem to do, how are we to choose between them? The answer grows out of an exposition of three levels of intention and feeling that are common in the experience of people.

A human being intends to do things. He is able to direct his body and to focus his intellectual activities. He chooses to spend the warm spring afternoon solving algebraic equations, or he decides to play ball instead. In either case he channels his powers into certain narrow limits. His feelings, however, are less subject to his control than are bodily and rational processes. By going outside on the spring day, he may open the door to excitement and fanciful passions. He may instead be opening the door to guilt and despondency because he has turned away from the actions that could prepare him for the algebra examination the next day. If he stays inside on the beautiful day, he might at first feel depressed as he hears the others shouting on the ball field. Yet, as he deliberately turns his attention to the challenge of unsolved math problems, he may feel a growing sense of well-being, and perhaps even excitement, as the intellectual work before him is mastered.

As he sets about his math assignment, his motives are mixed. He knows that the work must be done if he is to get a decent grade. He knows how he will feel if he does not study. What does he intend to do as he goes about his work? He plans to complete the assignment, and his sense of well-being is the result of this intended action. In the midst of his work another kind of feeling may break in on him—the sheer beauty of mathematics. Not everyone has this experience. An equation has symmetry and order; it reveals the harmony and structure of the universe; it can amaze one by its unity and perfection. This kind of emotion, however, is not the kind that one can control. One can hardly even open the door to it. Instead, it appears suddenly and is sensed rather than known. It may only be after the emotion has departed that one even is aware that it has been present. Yet, its presence was something pleasing and desirable.

How does worship fit into this human pattern of intention and emotional experience? There are three levels. First, there is the level of intention. When a person engages in an act of worship he may intend several things—to say "thank you" for life; to admit his failures; to deal with the potency that he encounters in time and space and in his relations with people; to maintain the life of his community at the level of moral value; to incorporate his children in a vision of reality. The second level is interwoven with the first. He also expects, at least part of the time, to experience emotions of tranquillity, acceptance, and inspiration. He hopes that this range of inner experience will come as a result of his intended acts.

There is a third level—a profound sense of life's meaning and harmony; an awareness of the world's beauty; a deep, intangible experience of "presence" that he cannot easily express. This third level may come as he engages in the first level, just as a sense of the beauty of mathematics may come while he is working problems. But the third level may also come at quite unexpected times—walking in the spring, driving home after an important event, listening to music, hearing the sounds of predawn, walking through a historical site.

Is this occasional, profound experience worship and not the other two levels? To say yes would be to say that worship takes place on rare occasions and in some people only. While some have wanted to answer this way, the main Christian tradition has answered the question by asserting that worship is both intended and unexpected, both subject to our control and independent of us, both ordinary and extraordinary. In one's immediate family the routines are part of the fabric of profound experience and emotion. When birthdays come, gifts are given more because of routine than because of intense, spontaneous generosity. Here again the routinized activity is carrier of a sustained relationship that may on some occasions include the unexpected, intense experience of love. Profound feelings of love might arise apart from these routinized relationships, but the greater likelihood is that the sensitivity and receptivity that open the way to overwhelming experiences are results of sustained relationships carried on at the level of rational intention.

So it is with worship. This human activity is another one that occupies that broad middle ground between utter spontaneity and absolute necessity. It is a routine that helps to keep alive a relationship within which profound experiences of ultimate concern can take place.

We can now speak specifically about form in worship and about feeling or religious experience. Worship as form, as slow dance, as symbol of social reality, as highly stylized symbolic act, is circumscribed by rules as is everything else about life—music and poetry, driving an automobile and making a living. Putting a child to bed at night has rules—with one child it is one kiss, one drink, and no song; with another it is no drink, one song, and two kisses—one on the lips and one on the nose, and in that order. The rules governing worship grow out of historic use and theological interpretation, are administered by the church, and interpreted by its theologians and scholarly authorities in the field of worship. There is, of course, latitude for local variation and flexibility; but in order for Christians always and everywhere to engage in common acts of ascribing worth to God, it is necessary that local custom and personal taste be shaped by ecumenical consensus.

While it is true that the validity of a form of worship does not depend upon our internal experience, it is also true that there must in time be some such experience or the form dies. What seems difficult for people today to experience is anything that might be called religious. They rarely sense their union with the world around or with divine spirit. With religious feeling absent, or at least weak, the form quickly becomes a mere repetition of words and rites that have lost their power.

It is wrong to use a service as the means of inducing that kind of feeling, for the intention of worship is not to induce feeling but instead to express it. If our services seem spiritless and dull, the explanation may well be that the forms we use, and the way we use them, have lost touch with the authentic experience of ultimate concern that we do have outside the church building, outside religious rite. The fault is not with our forms themselves; it is with our handling of the forms and our ways of teaching how they can express the depth of feeling that is present in contemporary life. A few days after the 1967 "ban-the-draft" riots in Oakland I heard a young woman from Australia, who had witnessed that violent episode, tell of the things that had happened.

On one day local police in a frenzy of fear beat help-less people bloodily even while these very people were obeying the commands to retreat that had been barked out over their heads. The pain and brutality were unforgivable, she reported. The next day minis-ters of the churches nearby went to the same place and on the streets that had run red with blood ad-ministered the sacrament of the body and blood of our Lord. The power of this act, said the witness, was irresistible. By using this strong symbolic form, which embodies the sense of the holy, they proclaimed their witness against man's inhumanity. At the same time they issued a call to reconciliation in the name of him whose way is won by sorrow and shame.

Are we, then, to wait for momentous occasions? Or is it possible for worship conducted in more or-dinary circumstances to be charged with power? How can we observe the rules and at the same time be in touch with authentic religious experience? To answer these questions we must turn to a consideration of the principles that determine liturgical style and form.

Liturgical
Style

During the 1968 plenary session of the Consultation on Church Union in Dayton, Ohio, I joined 150 people in the chapel of United Theological Seminary for a service that made present the cosmic wisdom the Christian faith proclaims. The preacher, Joseph A. Johnson, Jr., a bishop of the Christian Methodist Episcopal Church in Louisiana, delivered a profound and moving exposition of Galatians 2:11-21. Peter had been enjoying fellowship with gentile Christians who had not obeyed the Jewish ceremonial law. When men from Jerusalem came, he "drew back and separated himself" because he feared them. Paul affirmed that day the principle that men are justified by faith in Christ instead of by their works, and accused Peter of destroying the faith by refusing to sit at table with his Christian brothers whose race was different from his. By implication, Bishop Johnson's sermon denounced those who break fellowship over the works of men, whether it be baptism by immersion or ordination by a bishop; it denounced those who sever fellowship because of the accidents of race and position; it denounced every community that builds upon separateness rather than upon oneness in Jesus Christ.

Soon thereafter we moved to communion. William A. Benfield, Jr., head of the delegation of the Presbyterian Church in the United States, led the prayer:

Though we rebelled against your love, you did not abandon us in our sin, but sent to us prophets and teachers to lead us into the way of salvation. Above all, we give you thanks for the gift of Jesus your only Son, who is the way, the truth, and the life. In the fullness of time he took upon himself our nature; and by the obedience of his life, his suffering upon the Cross, and his resurrection from the dead, he has delivered us from the way of sin and death.

And we served communion to one another—Disciple to Episcopalian; layman to bishop; black man to white man; woman to man. At least for that hour we lost our self-esteem in all the forms it takes: denominational exclusiveness, theological systems, racism, the subtle conflict between sexes. For a little while we ceased being so eternally assertive, for the text that gathered us together was that verse in Galatians: "I have been crucified with Christ; it is no longer I who live, but Christ who lives in me; and the life I now live in the flesh I live by faith in the Son of God, who loved me and gave himself for me."

In this service of worship and in others that could also be described there is a particular style. If the liturgies that we carry out in our churches are to have any connection with real life as it ought to be, if they are to express persuasively the Christian vision of life, this style must be present.

The first quality to mark this style describes the mood of worship. It must, to use a phrase of Frederick Herzog's, "grasp the crude shape of what God has done in Christ." We have looked too much at Sallman's portraits of Christ and too little at Rouault's. Georges Rouault painted a picture of our Lord just before the crucifixion, stripped nearly naked, eyes closed, head drooping down. On either side of him is a soldier with red face and brutish features. The color is slapped on in slabs that are separated by bold strokes of black so that the impression is similar to the one given by some contemporary stained-glass windows. The effect is more like battle scenes on color television than like religious paintings. Here is a man who has gone without sleep for thirty-six hours, who has been severely manhandled, and left without food. Now, abandoned by everyone but a few helpless women, he slumps in complete exhaustion, too tired even to resist in this last five minutes before crucifixion. This picture is not beautiful; neither was the death of Christ, nor are the sins of pride and malice and stupidity and aggressiveness that put innocent men to death and deny hungry children their food. Somehow our services of worship must communicate this crude shape of what God has done in Christ and how it rescues us from ourselves.

Our human life does have qualities that can be described only by words like beautiful and peaceful. These attributes, too, belong in our worship. The ancient quality of "great thanksgiving" must continue to characterize our life together. Those who gather in the name of Jesus rightly anticipate that a sense of forgiveness and consolation will come. The glory of God and the glories of our daily life can properly be affirmed in the acts and words of worship.

All these qualities, however, must be conditioned by the prevailing mood of solemnity that results from the recognition of the crude shapes of human life and death. The combination of qualities for which I am calling is similar to that which emerged in the early life of the Christian community. At first the disciples were crushed by the death of their leader in whom they had placed their full trust. Then came the varied experiences of his continued life, and the despair was replaced by overwhelming excitement. Their gatherings were graced by hymn-singing, by great festivity, by the exuberance that marks the actions of those who have been freed from some over-powering tragedy. This rejoicing, however, was less than Christian, for it did not reckon adequately with the crucifixion. At this point the writings of Paul came to call the people back to a more restrained kind of rejoicing. Now their thanksgivings were to be made in the mood of penitence. Only those who experienced death with Christ could now share in the festal banquets of the resurrection.

In our time, too, there needs to be more of the sobriety and restraint that come when the grievous condition of the world is held steadily before our eyes. A great many of our standard church hymns must be set aside for partial retirement. Their texts and their musical qualities are gentle and comfortable, speaking of those times before the wars and famines of this century, before the full results of the industrial revolution, before the crisis of population, before the inhumanity of prejudice and race hatred, before the dehumanizing of our cities, before the breakdown of the great American experiment in equality for all men. It is right that we continue to use these hymns sometimes—in order to preserve part of our heritage and in order to maintain a witness to the possibility of that kind of tranquil and simple life. Yet, the prevailing tone of worship must be less that kind of peace and more that of tragic rejoicing.

The second major quality to be developed in our worship is that it must faithfully translate the gospel into the forms of contemporary life. In part this transition can be accomplished by the liturgical forms themselves. One Palm Sunday I was in a church in San Francisco where the gospel reading was Matthew 27:1-67, arranged to be read by several voices, one for each of the persons who speaks in the trial of Jesus. The lines spoken by the crowd were to be said by the congregation. With those around me I answered Pilate, "Let him be crucified." We do crucify him in our own ways today. We have real sin to confess and real forgiveness to beg for, and real promises to hope for. The language of worship and the liturgical forms themselves, while strong and graceful, must make explicit this sinfulness, this need of forgiveness, this desire to receive God's mercy.

61

No matter how skillfully the liturgical form is developed, however, this translation into the terms of modern life will have to be done primarily by means of the sermon. The liturgy as a whole suggests the mood and carries the sermon to its fullest potential development. Yet the sermon is the place where all comes clear. The world is full of easy-to-listen-to speeches about things we like. Hucksters who want our money say the flattering word; politicians who want our vote guess our prejudices and fears and shape their speeches accordingly; preachers whose ministry so often depends upon the good will of their constituents are tempted to say the soothing, healing word that we gladly hear. What we need more than we receive is the hard expertise that threatens us, that shakes the foundations of what we have always believed to be certain. The preacher must speak severely, exposing our past failures, showing to the world our pretenses, penetrating like the dentist's drill to the nerve that usually is so well protected we scarcely realize its presence.

This hard, serious speech has been proclaimed through the history of our Hebrew-Christian tradition. Long before Jesus spoke, men rose up to proclaim the Word of God. There would be, says B. D. Napier, a moment of "ecstatic concentration, of perception into the nature of things," of grasping what

God's will is. Then they would struggle to find language that could contain and convey this vision. In the speech of Isaiah and Amos and Jeremiah, of John and Jesus, the prophetic utterance would begin with an accusation of the people, "often extended and eloquent, commonly passionate and bitter." Then the prophet would speak the word of judgment, "brief, pointed, powerful, devastating, sometimes terrifyingly impersonal." In our own time, too, wise men arise in the spirit of biblical prophetism. When a prophet comes he says things that are hard for us to hear. His credentials are truth, wrought from an anguished concentration upon this world and its needs. Reading between the lines of daily life he finds the hidden Word of God and in his impassioned eloquence reads it to us letter by agonized letter.

How does such speech affect those who listen? The response, then and now, is a cry of pain. Hearing these hard words, we plead for something easier— and in the very act of calling for softer words we commit our rebellion against the God who speaks by the mouth of prophets. Speak to us what is favorable, we demand of the prophets. Be practical. Be sympathetic to our particular problems. Win us over by gentle persuasion rather than by denunciation. Wait until the time is right. Long ago Isaiah characterized this reaction when he called his countrymen

> a rebellious people,
> lying sons,
> sons who will not hear the instruction of the Lord;
> who say to the seers, "See not";
> and to the prophets, "Prophesy not to us what is right;
> speak to us smooth things,
> prophesy illusions,
> leave the way, turn aside from the path,
> let us hear no more of the Holy One of Israel."
>
> (Isaiah 30:9-10)

We had rather hear this smooth talk than the Word of God. Yet the prophet cannot heed us, for smoothness goes hand in hand with infidelity. It represents a loss of nerve. Those who wrestle with devils and angels win the battle only at the expense of smoothness.

How ought we respond to the prophet? We must have compassion for him, for he is driven by forces that torture him even as his words wound those who listen. The genuine prophet does not delight in inflicting pain. Those whom he wounds he loves, yet his love of God's word is even greater. We who sit at his feet must pity him even as we suffer from his rough and grating words. Yet we must urge him on, even though his prophesying brings pain to himself and to us. Only when prophets speak the truth is there hope for humanity. And we must be guided by the vision of that truth which the prophet proclaims, discerning in his words that which is true, finding ways of fulfilling God's will for us. When the prophet's words have scraped us bare and driven us to accomplish what he commands, they lose their power to wound. To our great surprise, the very words that before had been so hard to bear now sound smooth to our ears. In the way we had least expected our desire to hear smooth things is fulfilled.

The third quality to be developed as part of liturgical style is that the service in the church lead irresistibly to service in the whole life of man. This was the burden of the prophet:

> Wash yourselves; make yourselves clean;
>   remove the evil of your doings
>   from before my eyes;
> cease to do evil,
>   learn to do good;
> seek justice,
>   correct oppression;
> defend the fatherless,
>   plead for the widow. (Isaiah 1:16-17)

This sacrifice may take the form of generous private actions to alleviate poverty and suffering. Even more important is the institutionalized form that such intentions need to take. The structure of contemporary life is such that the most significant expressions of the energies of most of us are the institutions in which we work and achieve our goals for ourselves and society. These institutionalized extensions of human energy compound evil and perpetuate inequality and injustice; they make possible great good, as well. An insurance executive in Indianapolis devotes unreasonable and unprofitable blocks of time to counseling Negro clients who previously have been charged exorbitant fees for questionable coverage. A corporation executive in Louisville purchases a former parochial school building and turns it into a community center to serve people who live around his factory. A public school administrator in Seattle develops a program that promises simultaneously to relieve the growing financial cost of new school construction and the growing moral cost of de facto segregation. A white truck driver in Portland joins forces with a Negro blue-collar worker to develop an interracial scout troup so that boys of several races will come to know each other.

I do not know the reasons why these people chose to do what they did; it may be that some of them are not practicing Christians. This much is clear—their actions are the kind that Christians must perform. Only in this way will our faith be anything more than private solace and the means of escaping responsibility for the conditions of contemporary society.

It is becoming more difficult for churches to instruct their people about the ways of utilizing institutions for the advancement of the humane, for these institutions are part of what is being threatened by the social upheaval now taking place. The neighborhood concept of schools, the sovereignty of each political division—especially the incorporated suburbs of big cities—the supremacy of the profit motive, and the responsibility to protect the stockholder's interests are under attack. Those who know only this system and find their personal identity tied up with it cannot tolerate severe criticisms of it. They object to hearing the attacks, especially when those attacks come from presumably holy sources.

In such times the tendency is to insist that the church stay with the proper business of religion— which is interpreted to be the establishing of personal tranquillity and fortitude. The church is expected to be on the side of what has been inherited from the past, with the result that the whole emphasis is placed upon a private relationship to Jesus and the development of an attitude of trust toward him. Everything that moves in some other direction is rejected vigorously or sidestepped quietly. What is encouraged is talk about honor and morality, of decorum and regard for the law, of confident faith and thoughtful regard for those less fortunate than ourselves. This kind of talk may settle certain personal anxieties; *it will dampen no fires.*

The fourth quality to mark our liturgical style is that it must direct us to the source of strength. The collects in the *Book of Common Prayer* have one theme that appears repeatedly, a theme that also stands out in the Old Testament Psalms—the request that we be spared from many dangers. Today the dangers that surround us are in part natural, as they have always been. Even more they are the social and spiritual dangers that threaten to tear down our solemn resolves, that stifle our imagination and paralyze our efforts to remedy the evils of social life around us. Left to our own resources we stumble and soon fall. In these circumstances we must find support—from one another and from him who gave us life and will one day take us back to himself.

The most dangerous of all the enemies is despair. During coffee hour after church on the Sunday after Martin Luther King's funeral, one of the officers of the church, by race a Negro and by profession a barber, told me that once again his windows and the windows in the shop of his Jewish neighbor had been smashed out by rioters. Then he asked me if I, the professor, could suggest a way that would teach people not to do that any more. I hesitated, and he offered to give me until the next Sunday to come up with an answer. He knew and I knew that on the next Sunday there would be no answer. There can be none, because the old ones do not work and the new ones promise little improvement. We are in a desperate time, and people are using desperate means, some clutching the past and some grabbing for a future still beyond our reach. The frustration bursts out in uncontrolled violence.

How can we continue with love and justice, with militant nonviolence, with serious efforts to create a new society inspired by Christian virtues? How can we struggle against consistent defeat in our every venture without succumbing to despair? The only answer that can be given sounded forth in the sermon that the two of us had just heard that Easter Sunday. After a full discussion of the difference between the Easter faith and legendary resurrection stories in the gospel accounts, the preacher concluded with his own interpretation of our faith in this time. "We are not alone in an uncaring universe—alone with our sins and follies, our loss and grief and pain, our guns with telescopic sights, our unbridled hates and unreasoned judgments, our racism and nuclear power, our divided church with its traditional ways and conventional forms and reluctance to serve in the world. We are in the hands of God, and God is he who raised Christ Jesus from the dead." This faith proclaimed in sermon and celebrated in sacraments is what enables us to go about our work in times of violent passage.

Guidelines for the Free Tradition

My life has been lived in churches that worship according to the free tradition, in which minister and congregation are free to order their service and to choose the words, even of the most important prayers. In theory this kind of worship is designed to be open to the Holy Spirit, who is expected to inspire leaders and worshipers alike, but in practice the free tradition often deteriorates to banality and triviality. For this reason some people today would be very happy to abandon this approach to worship in favor of a fixed tradition in which the authority of the church as a whole, or at least of a denomination, determines liturgical order and the wording of prayers. It is obvious that the fixed liturgies have great strength and could be designed so as to manifest the liturgical style I am advocating.

I wish, however, to suggest a chastened mode of free worship, for this tradition has continuing value. It provides a flexibility that can be attained only with great difficulty in the fixed tradition, and it makes possible a directness and simplicity that are highly desirable in a time when people value those qualities so much. The free tradition fits the style and experience of a large segment of American Protestantism, for even churches such as the Methodist and Presbyterian, with their fixed liturgies for the administration of the sacraments, have ordinarily approached Sunday worship as though they were in the free tradition. One reason why their people have been known to resist the move toward sacramental worship is that such a move requires the change from free worship to prescribed.

The Consultation on Church Union is calling for the retention in the future of the liturgical traditions brought by the uniting churches. One of them is the free tradition that continues to have vigorous and committed supporters. To call the tradition free, however, does not mean the absence of rules for

procedure; even in this tradition there must be limitations and guidelines if practice is to be responsible.

The first principle is that the service be responsible
to the Christian consensus concerning the shape of the
liturgy. As long as what we are conducting is to be
called worship, it must have some relation to the
views of the whole church as to what constitutes
worship that is worthy and legitimate. Early in the
history of Christianity the service of Word and Sacrament was established as the normative form of Christian worship. During the course of the church's life
that tradition has been divided into variations or uses,
some going back into ancient times and some coming
into existence since the sixteenth-century Reformation. In our own time scholars from the various
traditions are rediscovering the common base upon
which all our variations are built, and they are finding
new ways of expressing that unity even while pre-
serving the right to and desirability of variety in
forms.

The most satisfactory way of expressing responsible
relations to the Christian consensus, in its classical,
denominational, and contemporary manifestations, is
by means of *common order*. By this phrase I mean
the establishing of the sequence of major parts so as
to correspond to Christian consensus and to provide
the theological continuity that must be considered
essential to worship that is called Christian. Stripped

to its bare minimum, common order consists of three elements—scripture, sermon, and supper. If any of these elements is missing, the service is defective; with these elements present, the service has adequate historical and theological continuity with the church's life and faith. Common order includes not only certain elements but also a certain sequence, the one that has been followed by most of the church since early in Christian history.

The first element in common order is the reading of scripture. The Bible records the experiences with God of a particular people whose wrestlings with him began some two thousand years before Christ. Written over a long period of time, the separate manuscripts that form the Bible vary widely in the clarity of their language and the fullness of their revelatory power. Just as the panes of glass in a stained-glass window transmit sunlight in differing degrees, so the various books of the Bible transmit the knowledge of God in varying degrees. Some portions, while useful for private study, have little place in the church's public worship. Leaders of the service must therefore exercise great care in selecting portions to be read in the hearing of the congregation. Sunday by Sunday they should present those portions of the biblical record which are of greatest help in revealing God's presence with his people in the ages long ago. Yet, leaders must take pains to use the Bible extensively. Over a period of months or years the reading in public worship should be representative of the entire Bible, giving samples of its varied content, portraying the several styles of material, depicting its grand scope.

Just as the scripture readings tie the service to the people of God throughout all ages, so the sermon ties the service to the contemporary world of human action. It properly uses idioms of today, strives for clarity of thought and contemporaneity of illustration. Because communication is so important, leaders of worship will be willing to use varied styles—such as dialogues, dramatic readings, and music—if by so doing they can help people see more clearly how God is present in their own realm of experience. Because the sermon is to help people render their thanksgiving to God at the communion table, the preacher will speak with eloquence and persuasiveness, dealing with the ground of skepticism and superficiality that so pervade contemporary culture. Remembering that he stands in the prophetic line that began long before Christ, he will speak courageously about the crises of our time. Yet the preacher will remember that the privilege of his position is dependent upon his faithfulness to the revelation transmitted through Scripture, Christian tradition, and his own wrestlings with God.

The third element of the common order has four

parts; three are essentially action and the fourth is a prayer that puts into words the meaning that is implicit in the other three. The *offertory* is the bringing of gifts from the life of the people. To the traditional elements of bread and wine are added monetary contributions, all of which represent the daily life of the people there assembled. These elements placed on the table express the self-giving of these people in grateful response to God for the life that he has given. This intention is stated in the *communion prayer* in which a minister sums up the congregation's thanksgiving for life and for the new life given by Christ. The *breaking of bread*, following the example of Jesus at his last supper with the disciples, strengthens the memorial, for it ties this service to Jesus' self-sacrifice of long ago. Then comes the *communion* when a portion of the people's offering to God is returned to them as the bearer of his presence and love, renewed and intensified.

A second major principle for guiding free worship is that the service be responsive to the life of our time. Important as the past is to the life of the present, we do not live back then. The styles and moods of our time must somehow be sensed by those who plan and conduct worship. By their personal bearing and by the service itself they must express this sensitivity to the way of life now. This responsiveness, however, does not require shifts in the common order. By

means of the words that are said and sung, by the
kind of music used, and by the kind of ceremony
followed this response to contemporary life is
manifested.

Prayers in the service should express this sensitivity
to contemporary life, with petitions and intercessions,
confessions and thanksgivings rising out of current
life-experience. The literary style of prayer must be
considered carefully, too, for we are in a transitional
time. The gradual change in English usage, which
has required that new translations of the Bible be
made, now is bringing about a change in the language
of prayer. Not only are the archaic pronouns and
verbal forms falling into disuse, but other archaic
speech patterns are also being set aside. The complex,
artfully balanced sentence, reminiscent of Latin con-
structions, is giving way to the brisk sequence of
clauses and phrases that characterize good English
usage of our time. Although the classical English
language of prayer will continue to be a heritage to
cherish, the newer forms of speech will increasingly
be used. Those responsible for leading public prayer
must work at their style so they can use current
speech habits skillfully, gracefully, and articulately.

Responsiveness to contemporary life can also be
manifested by reading, as a transition between the
ancient readings and the contemporary word of the
sermon, a significant writing from the body of Chris-

tian literature that has developed since the days of the apostles. The fathers of the Church, the reformers of the sixteenth century, the great theologians of our own age, the preachers and poets and essayists of recent decades have written significant literature that is neither prayer nor sermon. This kind of material could be read in a service of worship on special occasions or during one season of the church year. These contemporary readings must be chosen with great and good judgment. Modesty of tone and style, aptness of phrasing, and strength of content are qualities to be sought. Shock value should be avoided, for it tends to destory the effects that are sought by the incorporation of such new material. Although such readings will generally come from the writings of people who are clearly within the Christian tradition, on some occasions they might be chosen from sources admittedly not Christian. In every case these readings must have some discernible connection to the understanding of God and life that is manifested in scripture. That collection of writings is the anchor which the church has established; or we might say, the stake to which we are tied. For that reason when a contemporary reading is used it should be added to the readings of Scripture, not replace them.

The music used in worship also contributes to this responsible connection to the contemporary world. Music is an expressive form that conveys emotional and organic experiences about life and death, with all their implications. The means of expression change from generation to generation, each one finding new melodies, new rhythms, new harmonic patterns. Yet the function of music, whether in worship or outside, is constant—to articulate experience that ordinary words by themselves cannot express. The church must be open to forms of music as they appear and learn how they can be incorporated into liturgical life. Music chosen for use in the liturgy must help worship by taking people closer to the experience and understanding of the reality that supports worship. At the same time it must be close enough to the tastes and likes of the congregation that communication with them is possible. Perhaps most important is that music used by the church must be more than amateurish imitations of the contemporary; rather, it must represent the idioms of the time at their strongest and best. Thus, says Norman O'Conner, the contemporary composer of liturgical music has to seek out "the depth that flows in a line from Armstrong to a Rod Levitt, from a Leadbelly to a Dylan, from an Ellington to a Mingus, from a Gershwin to a Lalo Shiffrin." Obviously, there is no one musical style that represents the moods and tastes of contemporary life, and much of the music being composed now is not going to survive. Yet our time is a new one, and there is great vitality in many of the new compositions. Here, as in so many other aspects of life, the informed judgments of the community at large, but especially of its most sensitive people, are very important. We must listen to their compositions and examine their reviews in order to choose the music to be used in our churches for the worship of God.

The third guideline for free worship is that the major communion prayer must combine qualities from both the free and the fixed traditions. I have spent a quarter of a century listening to impromptu communion prayers delivered every Sunday. When the entire service is weak—poor music, poor preaching, shallow prayers—one scarcely notices a faulty communion prayer. When the other portions of a service are strong, however, the communion prayer must be strong, too, or the contrast is very evident. There is much to be said in favor of using an invariable text as is the common practice in most of Christendom. The congregation is protected from the idiosyncrasies of the minister, and theological adequacy is assured for the prayer. A fixed text preserves a tone and provides for a climactic development in the service. Yet the invariable text, even with seasonal prefaces, is necessarily generalized and thus incapable of reflecting as fully as often is desirable the mood and intention of the congregation on the particular Sunday that the service is in use.

By combining free and fixed elements into one

prayer, however, strengths of the two traditions can be preserved and weaknesses overcome. Because of its flexibility of form and style, the free prayer would express thanksgiving for life in all of its variety, richness, and changeableness. Our sinfulness and concern for all mankind could be incorporated into this free prayer. Because life is so varied, this prayer, more than any other part of the service, would require freedom from fixed texts and forms, and freedom for full expression of the life that God gives to his people.

The second part of the prayer by its very nature calls for greater uniformity of language. Its purpose is to call to remembrance Jesus and his sacrificial life and to pray for the "gifts and graces" of his presence. While these sentiments can be phrased in varied language, there is good reason to restrict the range. Because the theology involved can be complex and difficult to express precisely, a pattern of words, once developed, should be used repeatedly. Even this prayer might be in the tradition of free prayer—that is, worded by the minister. Such work, however, should be done with great deliberation and prayer, over a period of time in the peace of his study, and the results committed to paper. This is no time for impromptu praying. As normal practice this fixed part of the prayer should include the words of the institution of the Lord's Supper, which has been a part of the memorial act of the prayer since early in Christian history.

If these suggestions were followed, the communion prayer would be outlined in this way:

(a) Dialogue (minister and congregation)

(b) Free prayer (minister): thanksgiving for the life God gives, petition, intercession

(c) Ascription of praise (unison or choir)

(d) Fixed prayer (minister): remembrance, including the words of institution, and petition for the renewing of Christ's presence

(e) Dedication of life to God and to one another (unison or minister)

(f) Lord's Prayer (unison)

The one part of this complex prayer that would change weekly is the free prayer. The dialogue, ascription of praise, and Lord's Prayer would be used regularly and permanently. The fixed prayer of remembrance and petition and the dedicatory prayer could be changed from time to time—perhaps for each major season of the church year, or perhaps at the beginning of each new church year.

The Lord's Supper is an action with a specific meaning suggested by Jesus himself. The action is performed by the service as a whole, and the meaning is expressed in the communion prayer. A service that moves swiftly and directly from scripture, through sermon, to the call to offering and the communion prayer has great dramatic strength and devotional force. When this kind of service is being conducted there is something about it that drives toward consummation, leaving little time for the distractions that are so common in services paced more leisurely.

The hardest element to incorporate in this direct-style service is the long prayer of intercession for ourselves and the world, often called the pastoral prayer. Yet the sentiments that this prayer traditionally includes must be in the service, for the church must call the needs of the whole world into its life of prayer to God. The practical problem is one of placement. Sometimes it is put between the lessons and the sermon. While this prayer does suit the heralding of the Word, it breaks the connection that seems to be so right, the connection between the readings and the sermon. A second place for the intercessions is following the sermon where they can be the response to the entire act of heralding the Word. The problem here is that the flow from the sermon to the offertory is interrupted. The sermon is a call to commitment as well as the heralding of the Word, and it needs to lead directly into the offertory summons. If a long prayer appears here it breaks the sequence. If the prayer is strong it makes the offertory and communion anticlimactic. Thus, some people put the intercessions early in the service. Yet the congregation is hardly ready to engage in such a long period of prayer that early in their time together.

The logic of the service leads to one conclusion: there should be only one prayer of any length and importance in the service, and that one prayer should be prayed at the communion table following the gathering and presentation of gifts. Here should be gathered up the thanksgiving, confession, petition, dedication, and adoration of the congregation. Here the full force of the Word proclaimed should be expressed by the actions of the people (in the offering) and by the words of their appointed leader. On Sundays when the full service of Word and Sacrament is celebrated this long prayer would include specific thanksgiving for the new life in Christ, an act of memorial, and petitions for the renewal of his presence in our lives. On Sundays when the full sacrament is not administered, the prayer would make only minimal reference to this specifically eucharistic and sacramental portion of the communion prayer.

Despite the logic of this practice, I hesitate to recommend it. Ministers with insufficient liturgical knowledge or literary skill to put this full meaning into words will deliver communion prayers as trite as their pastoral prayers now are. The private interests of the minister might easily become dominant, crowding out the proper concerns for the whole world and for the memorial of Christ that this act performs. Yet risks like these are present wherever the practice

83

of free prayer has been encouraged. At its best free prayer has a beauty, relevance, and power that prescribed prayer rarely attains. But free prayer is rarely at its best.

Two courses of action seem feasible considering these several factors. One is to maintain the separation of the two long prayers, in this way assuring the presence of intercessions and the theological integrity of the communion prayer. In general practice, the pastoral prayer should come before the sermon, for in this place it cannot usurp the emotional feeling or liturgical function that must be reserved for the communion prayer. Once the sermon is over, the service moves to the table, and the strong response of the congregation to the Word is expressed in the offertory procession, communion prayer, and sacrament of bread and wine.

The second course of action is to combine intercessions with the communion prayer but with a preface of biddings. Before the dialogue begins, the minister would announce the concerns that should be included in the prayer—world conditions, the state of the church, the needs of people in the congregation. He would then begin the dialogue. In the free prayer that follows he would not again mention the biddings, but he might include a formula of reference: "And we pray especially for those whose names and needs we today remember."

A fourth general guideline for the ordering of worship in the free tradition is that services should combine variety and repetition, excitement and sobriety. The free tradition has always advocated that there be variety in the words used in worship. In current practice this principle has deteriorated to the insistence that the language of prayers always be different from that of the previous week, that hymns and musical responses should not be repeated too quickly, that efforts should be made to rotate readings and other parts of the service so that no one remembers the last time something was used. While this kind of variation has some value and is probably better than having none at all, it has serious limitations too. One is that there is less variety than one might think. The tendency is for every service to seem the same even though the words and tunes used are different. Dullness sets in, and dullness in church is as deadly as in any other social group. This kind of variation, furthermore, thwarts the development of one of the most important kinds of congregational participation. When the text of the service changes every week and the congregation is expected to participate vocally, the obvious consequence is dependence upon printed words, but not all the congregation reads. Children in the early grades of school cannot keep up with the written word that quickly. Older persons, who might be able to, often are not willing to.

A combination of long-cycle and short-cycle patterns provides variety that is liturgically significant and at the same time practical. Short-cycle changes make possible the flexibility that is needed in order for services to adapt to variations of emphasis. Long-cycle changes permit the congregation to grow accustomed to phrases and patterns of response, thus reducing the dependence upon printed materials. They also permit the variety to be more complete. By combining devotional elements and congregational participation into harmonious patterns that are used several weeks at a time, it is possible to change substantially the mood of worship even while the common order is unchanged. By being conservative in changes of order and imaginative in periodical changes of supporting elements, we can provide a sense of continuity and familiarity and a sense of excitement and variety. At least, there should be no question of boredom. At all times, however, decorum should be maintained. The church at worship on Sunday is an affair of public nature, requiring restraint and sobriety even while manifesting vitality and excitement.

The principles described throughout this chapter would result in a service that is brisk, dramatically strong, and theologically adequate. It would begin with a sentence from Scripture or some other brief statement that asks the congregation to worship God, to which might be added a prayer requesting his help in this act of worship. A hymn setting forth God's greatness and power could be sung or similar sentiments be stated in a unison or antiphonal reading. A combination of these elements might sometimes be used as long as leaders of the service avoided overloading this portion. These introductory elements should be planned as a unit in order to express the mood that prevails in the season of the year when the service is conducted.

Chosen leaders of the service would then move quickly to the reading of Scripture. When more than one passage is read, and this should be normal practice, a brief interlude might separate them—a hymn or brief musical text, or a response said by the congregation. If there is a reading from sources other than the Bible, it would come at this point. When the pastoral prayer is a separate element, it would follow the readings. After a theme hymn or anthem, the minister would preach. The sermon might be followed by a period of silence in order to encourage the congregation to meditate upon the Word and to appropriate its implications.

A leader of the service, perhaps a layman, would then invite the congregation to present themselves as a living sacrifice to God, and the gifts of the people would be brought forward to the communion table (after being collected in some appropriate way). This presentation might be accompanied by a hymn or doxology of praise sung by the congregation. It might be possible for this hymn to be the same one used at later portions of the thanksgiving response. In this way the several parts of the service conducted at the table are clearly bound together. A leader of the service might at this time read a passage of Scripture that serves as warrant for the communion and invitation to participate. When intercessions and communion prayer are combined, the minister would announce the themes for inclusion in the prayer and then begin the dialogue. At the close of the prayer the bread would be broken before the people and the cup distributed to the servers who in turn minister to the congregation. The final act would be a dismissal of the people with the commission that they be responsible servants of Christ. During the communion service there could be a hymn or anthem that depicts one of the several meanings closely related to communion, and a hymn could conclude the service.

This outline permits wide variation in detail and manner of celebration. Consequently, each minister, in consultation with his congregation, is free to adapt it to the particular circumstances that must be met. In some cases the bare minimum, performed in direct and intimate style, is the only right way to administer the service of Word and Sacrament. In other circumstances, especially on festival Sundays and in places where the church building is of grand style, the service must be planned with greater fullness of text and manner of performance. Instead of piano accompaniment of congregational singing, organ and brass ensemble; instead of the simple entrance by leaders of the service, a solemn procession by choir and other leaders; instead of street clothes worn by leaders, vestments that have been developed for use in the church.

The form of the free tradition that has been advocated in this chapter is simple and conservative. Even so, its inauguration in a congregation might create the impression of radical change. Gone would be some of the customary elements—some of the short, devotional prayers would probably be removed; some of the musical responses might be eliminated. It is true that the communion prayer is probably more extended than is the custom in most free churches, and the provision for congregational participation in that prayer would call for substantial revision in current practice. All this change would give the impression that the service had been made more complex. Yet what I am recommending is simpler in structure, more direct in movement, and probably shorter in elapsed time than most orders of worship that it would replace. I have avoided the suggestions often made that spontaneous dialogue take the place of sermon and congregational sentence prayers the place of the major pastoral prayer of intercession. Recommendations of that kind are more frequent now than they used to be, frequently growing out of extended experimentation, trial, and revision. It may be that my group of recommendations are for a service that will last only during an interim when we pass from one form of worship to another far different from what we now know.

We do live in a time of transition that includes the relatively normal change in musical and artistic tastes, in attitudes and experiences. With the advent of television and the remarkable developments of transportation and computerized processes, the normal changes are accelerated and intensified. Generational gaps and cleavages between social classes seem to be greater now than has been true previously in American life. What this means for worship is that the older ways may well have to give way to forms and styles that we cannot yet forecast. While experimentation is very much in order for the new forms to be discovered, this casting about for the forms of the future must be undertaken with great care. It probably will be conducted most of the time away from the regular Sunday assembly, for where small, closely knit groups gather in intensive fellowship, experimentation in styles of relationship, including worship, is possible and desirable. In time what is discovered there can be shared with the larger and less flexible liturgical assembly.

Experimentation should grow out of new and enriched experience rather than impatience or despair, frustration or anger. It should be carefully conceived and marked by three criteria, which James F. White has expounded. Those who experiment must learn from history both the mistakes that might be avoided and an understanding of the present and its needs. Experimentation must be well founded theologically, giving proper expression to the meaning of life, of worship, of reality itself. Experimentation must be pastorally relevant, connected to the life that people today really are living, recognizing its diversity and its breadth and depth.

All the elements that have been discussed—music, readings, sermon, communion—when included in a service of worship tend to lose their separate identities by being incorporated into a larger art form that expresses ultimate concern in symbolic form. To accomplish this function the service must avoid distracting and irrelevant elements. What is included in the service must be kept because it articulates clearly and powerfully this experience of the "depth of being," of ultimate concern. Unfortunately, artistic genius is doled out to humanity in differing measure. Almost every person can whistle a tune of some kind, but only a few composers are able to create great art. A larger portion of humanity can enter into the artistic process of performing a composition that someone has created. An even larger segment of the race can join the process by listening and thus entering into the musical experience. The same kind of human variation is true when it comes to the carrying out of worship as high art. The creation of powerful liturgical form requires insight and skill that are not the possession of every pastor, choir director, or worship committee. Thus, leaders of every congregation must be willing to look to the prototypes of worship that are emerging across the nation when the combination of circumstances gives rise to a form of worship that combines effectively the principles I have articulated.

Weekend
and Holy Day

All that I have said about liturgical style and the free tradition, about the revivification of basic wisdom and its transmission to the new generation, presupposes that people are in church on Sundays and that what they find there is convincing to them. But church is the one place they seem not to be. We need to understand why, and then we must take a position concerning this fact of our generation. Finally, we must develop the appropriate course of action for the immediate future.

One reason for their absence has been referred to earlier—a general loss of confidence in the factual truth of Christian claims. Even when the faith and its liturgical forms are considered to be high art, they must be believed in if they are to involve people in them significantly. This belief is wavering; a new mood has arisen, and it affects church people as much as anyone else. By the word mood I mean the state of mind that a person simply has and expresses in everything that he does. Mood is the way one feels about himself, his world, and their meaning. It is made up of presuppositions or rules-of-thumb by which he understands his experiences. While it is to some degree connected with one's reasoning powers, mood is mainly nonrational. It is developed by natural and environmental factors and is usually accepted without question and rarely subjected to scrutiny. Thus mood is very important in all human activity, for, as much as anything else, it gives rise to everything that we do. Yet, because mood is unexamined, it is difficult to describe accurately.

The mood in our time is characterized by preoccupation with this world of natural human life in a strange universe. Earlier in this century it was still possible to develop a vigorous battle between philosophers holding idealist views and those holding realist views. No longer is this so. The prevailing point of view in the philosophy journals today is suggested in an essay by Y. H. Krikorian published in a volume honoring William Ernest Hocking. Hocking had insisted that there must be a "universal other Mind" because only when something is known by someone can it exist. For the world to be, there must be that One who knows it. In contrast to this view, Krikorian insists that there is no need to resort to this "cosmic Mind" in order to account for nature or the universality of our judgments of value. Hocking's assertion, Krikorian holds, invites a question why this universal Mind exists, to which Hocking had given the answer that here we encounter that mystery, that "sense of wonder without which human existence ceases to be human." Krikorian's retort: "One need not discard this mood, but why not apply it to Nature? If we are going to end in mystery, nothing is gained by going beyond Nature."

This mood infects other philosophers; it is far advanced among theologians; it infects church people as well. When they experience a violent storm they may say that God sends the wind to speak to them and that he stops the fury when his purposes are fulfilled. It is more likely, however, that they will accept the weather bureau's explanation for the storm and its sudden ending. What for the ancient Hebrews would have been a powerful demonstration of their God's might is for a contemporary congregation a terrifying experience explainable by scientific information. If prayers are offered, they are not thanks-givings that God has spared his people but requests that in his mercy he would minister to those who have suffered loss. Modern man may still feel that God is the source of all things and the ruler of history, but he turns to science for detailed explanations of particular events.

The effect upon worship is devastating because the worshiper's conception of the meaning of life shapes what he is able to do when he comes together with his fellows. Wilbur M. Urban states the issue well when he asserts that the liturgy and the creed that is set within it must "be taken as an integral whole." The liturgy is "a form of sound words," whose theological meaning is stated in its creed. Urban analyzes the Nicene Creed into three kinds of propositions: metaphysical assertions, which speak of the being and nature of God; cosmological propositions, which speak of the relation of God to his world through creation and redemption; and historical propositions, which speak of divine actions in time. His conclusion is that this total world view must be accepted if one is to worship God.

But this world view is what contemporary Christians and non-Christians find unreal or which they can no longer affirm with the confidence that Urban could manifest not many decades ago. Some continue to walk through the paces of church life, but the intensity of involvement is gone. Even though they may not understand their uneasiness, they sense that all is not right. Others resolve the tension by leaving the church so that the reminders of the former mood will no longer confront them. Still others, recognizing the social values of the church, participate freely in the nonliturgical phases of its program. Since they do not have to repeat the traditional language of worship they can live their this-worldly lives without explicit compromise.

A second factor that helps account for the falling away from the church is the rising importance of art as a means of dealing with the inner life. Although the field of aesthetics continues to be one marked by some confusion, it is clear that art and religion are somehow closely related. Each in some way connects a person with the "absolute," however that might be defined. Each has a certain detachment from the detail of passing events. Each is a symbol of the way that things affect a man. Each helps a man to attain "a sublime calm within the very passions of life." Art and religion reveal the patterns of our inner life and vitality; they shape our subjective being, that "most intimate 'Reality' that we know." It is true that aesthetic experience and religious experience can be distinguished, at least in phenomenological analysis. Yet in daily life that distinction is often not realized. It is easy for one to take the place of the other.

Especially is this likely when religion deteriorates or when public confidence in religion declines. Then it is that people begin to move toward the arts, which in their own way provide for dealing with one's inner life. Thus a university professor states that the symphony is as important to him as the church. A church that is half empty on ordinary Sundays is filled when a Bach cantata is sung. People who would hesitate to profess faith enter a religious art exhibition with works that demonstrate profound feelings of the nature of reality.

Earlier I described the way that religion becomes high art in the gradual developing of human experience. I said that it makes little difference whether people consider the liturgy in which they participate to be cosmic myth or high art, for in either case they were telling the same stories and entering into the same vision of reality. The problem that I am talking about here is not this shift from cosmic myth to high art as the explanation of the nature of worship. Rather it is the shift away from participation in worship, however the liturgy is interpreted, to other types of art appreciation and aesthetic experience.

A third factor is the emergence of a new weekend pattern of life. In a widely read family magazine Farrell Cross devoted four pages to describing "pocket vacations," which are so different from the work week that a good weekend can be as invigorating as an ordinary, poorly planned, month-long vacation. In the entire article, in which Cross describes work projects, adult education, sporting activities, and specialized travels, there is only one reference to church —he suggests that some families find a broadened outlook by visiting churches of denominations other than their own on one or two Sundays a month. The effect of this new weekend pattern on churchgoing is clear to anyone who examines attendance records. The pocket vacation, no matter how spent, is fun; it is refreshing; it provides a way of escaping from the clamor of work and regular responsibilities. The trend underway cannot be reversed.

A fourth factor is the change taking place in the patterns by which people arrange time. Rural life has always been arranged according to an annual cycle— a time to prepare the ground and a time to harvest. In the city manufacturing and trade have gone on the year around. Even though public school has had a certain prominence in setting family schedules, the commercial processes have been more important. Because every week was the same as every other, every Sunday was also a repetition of every other one. Now, the annual cycle is ever more prominent, in cities as well as in the country. Retail merchants have developed a schedule that follows an annual cycle— back-to-school, Halloween, Thanksgiving, Christmas, January sales. Whether they are churchgoers or not, families are aware of the traditional church festivals and their effect upon the patterning of time. Vacations for the family are more important and break up the year more than once was true. The sports schedule on TV and in the schools follows the annual cycle.

The result is that while the seven-day week continues to divide up time—for work and school and church program—the annual cycle is now coming into greater prominence. People who no longer work at the same pace every week, but vary the pattern throughout the year, see little reason to attend church simply because the day is Sunday. Now the tendency is to go on a particular Sunday because it falls in a part of the annual cycle when churchgoing seems to be the thing to do.

It is too early to discern with confidence what will be the shape of American life and thought in the future. We live in an interim that will some time lead into a new flowering of the life of man, and toward that new era we must work. Philosophers and theologians and scientists must push forward as vigorously as money and imagination and discovery will permit until that time when a new intellectual consensus is created, when a new culture as universal as scientific civilization now is binds all mankind together, when there emerges a way of combining known facts and ultimate mysteries that unites man

100

instead of separating him from his fellows as the religions now do. We are far from achieving that new world for which we long. The institutions of the past are still our homes and will be as far into the future as we now can see. What we need, therefore, is a provisional design that maintains our contact with the past and openness to the future while remaining viable in this ambiguous era. The church, too, must find its way, and for its provisional design I am proposing two elements: paradigmatic story as the approach to truth, and imaginative use of the Christian calendar as the approach to contemporary life styles.

During 1967 a select group of poets and theologians held a seminar at the National Cathedral in Washington, D. C., on the theme "Myth in Religion and Literature." The theologians meant by myth "an all-inclusive, complex set of stories within whose framework persons . . . live their lives." They argued that once people lived by their myths but that now this pattern of thought is broken and meaningless. The poets disagreed with the theologians. For them myth meant any of the strongly representative stories "which articulate human experiences, including the religious." The poets insisted that these paradigmatic stories continue to be true to experience and that they are genuine expressions of the life of people today.

Myths in the sense of representative stories provide a way by which we can pattern our response to the manifold experiences that come to us. This world in which we live is a complicated place, and the complexity grows as our scientific discoveries advance. What to a small child seems so simple soon is revealed to be elaborate. So it is with our knowledge of reality. Some people can wander along from day to day without formulating the diversity of experience into patterns of meaning that would enable them to move about with some sense of direction and purpose. These patterns of meaning, of course, are many in number, for each of us puts things together in his own fashion, but they can be summarized into two groups.

What is man? A combination of chemical elements organized so that certain processes can be carried out. That is one way of organizing our experiences of mankind. The other way begins with man's capacity to think and feel, to move and create, and then deals with what can be listened to by stethoscopes and looked at by X rays. What is the universe? Some affirm that nature is to be understood as physical process inexorably moving onward toward that time when its energies have been depleted. Other people affirm that man is surrounded by a sphere of wisdom, that the best clue to the nature of reality is man's spirit rather than his body. The trouble is that we cannot prove which way of interpretation is right. Owen Barfield talks about two kinds of knowledge. Put a person behind the wheel of a car and teach him to manipulate the knobs and levers until the car runs; that is dashboard knowledge. Put up the hood and teach a man what makes the car run, and that is engine knowledge. Most of what we know about life and the universe is dashboard knowledge. We may know that if we do certain things certain results will occur, but most of the time, even in the natural sciences, we don't know why. The question, then, is this: Which kind of dashboard knowledge works— the one that sees the universe as being bounded by cosmic wisdom, or the one that affirms the lifelessness of space? The answer of the Christian tradition is that the view that begins with cosmic wisdom is the effective one. This view does not create nuclear explosions nor build dams on rivers, but it does make the life of man better by helping him overcome his selfishness, his cruelty, his blindness to the needs of others. The vision of cosmic wisdom surrounding us makes it possible for us to live a life that is full of promise in the days of youth, full of wisdom in the days of old age, and content to fall to the ground and die so that the whole life of man might advance toward a future with meaning.

The Christian patterning of life's meaning is cast in story form with Jesus of Nazareth the dominant figure. The many episodes where he appears, the many teachings that he delivers, are all of a kind—they convey to us an understanding of what really is and of what really counts. Though we cannot put our conviction in reasoned discourse as powerful as these stories, what we mean by them is that behind the appearances, beneath the structures, inside the bodies of this universe, there is the same spirit that we meet in Jesus. This spirit suffers and survives, it labors and gives birth, it dies and rises again, it loves and hates and perseveres, it grows and matures; and if it must have a name, it is the God and Father of our Lord Jesus Christ. Such a way of talking is neither scientific nor historical. It is preconceptual or foundational, orienting us to reality, establishing us in our life, liberating us for living in love. Just as the poets told the theologians, so we must say: These stories are no figure of speech; they tell the truth.

This approach to truth stands between two others that are widely followed within the church's life today. On one side are Christians who claim with considerable certainty the literal truth of the representative stories and the cosmic wisdom that I have described. My frequent references to high art and cosmic myth, to poetry and paradigmatic story they reject as denials of the gospel and its claims upon man's mind and spirit. Many of these Christians are aware of the immense scientific and philosophical problems that make it difficult to believe in the literal truth of traditional theology. They have, however, found a way of maintaining a double truth: Science and faith are accepted with equal confidence. On the other side are Christians who doubt all the truth claims of theology. Stripping away legend and super- stition, mythical world view and liturgical invention, they reveal factual emptiness at the center of the faith. They are counterparts in the field of theological analysis to theoretical physicists in another field, who have stripped away the solid surface of the world only to discover that subatomic matter eludes their grasp.

I find myself very close to the position that Helmut Kuhn ascribes to Ernst Cassirer. An observer watches a piece of cloth being woven on a loom—but he can see neither the weaver who is doing the work nor the loom on which the cloth is taking shape. All that the observer can know about the unseen he must discover and imagine as he studies the pattern in the cloth, which ever grows bigger. In Cassirer's system the cloth, which we can know, is the symbolic form—art, science, religion, language. What we cannot know are the exact nature of the real world and the exact nature of the creative force, which somehow brings life-forms into being. Just out of sight on either hand these unknowns are hovering. In the flux of experi- ence, from which the symbolic forms are created, we see a shadow of that reality which scientists and philosophers call actual. In the creativity we detect something that resembles the Christian God. We peer into the shadows to detect the nature of the real world and, like Moses, to see God face to face. Never is our effort successful; always we come back to the forms that the creativity of man produces. Yet as we do so it is with a confidence that in this human work we detect the marks of what really is, and in this confidence we go about the life that must be lived.

The traditional calendar of Christianity is closely tied to the narratives of Jesus' life, which are so important to the approach to truth which I am suggesting. From Advent to Pentecost the church follows the Nazarene and is caught up in the mystery of his life and presence through all time. The stories of his birth and life, his miracles and mighty deeds, his suffering and death, his resurrection and his enthronement are told with adoring wonder and affirmed with joy. Christians find their own lives illumined and impowered by this annual recitation of salvation's history. In the midst of a natural world that moves relentlessly, threatening our hopes, we find in that history a way of making peace with ourselves and the universe. Yet the traditional calendar of Christianity is little used by many Protestants—because of the iconoclasm of our Calvinist ancestors, because of our ignorance, because we have been little moved by some of the traditional ceremonies. What we now must do is develop a form of the Christian calendar and style of celebration that does for our generation what once was done by the older Christian calendar with its ways.

The place to begin is with major dates that already are accepted in general life, infusing them with appropriate content and building around them the proper supporting structure of celebrations: two seasons come from the traditional Christian year and one from the rhythm of secular life. This last one is not so much a date as it is a time of year—the ending of summer and the beginning of fall. For most people the crucial happening for establishing schedules is the beginning of school, and at that point the pattern of life returns to normal. This season is recognized in churches by varied promotional programs. While these institutional calls to duty serve a useful function, they often are thin and thus contribute less than they might to the incorporation of people into the community of faith. What is needed is a closer tie between the natural rhythm of beginning again and the fundamental content of the Christian faith.

The best suggestion yet made for this season is that of A. A. McArthur, who recommends that the starting point for the Christian year be a "festival of creation" on the first Sunday of October, followed by several Sundays when the dominant theme is thanksgiving for the whole creation. Here is a strong beginning for the annual cycle—one that ties together that sense of new beginnings associated with the start of school, the harvest rejoicings of Thanksgiving Day, and a celebration of God the Father, Creator and Sustainer of all things. If the preaching schedule takes full advantage of the season, and if other parts of congregational life are planned accordingly, members of the church will be strengthened in their faith and converts won.

The season of creation is not unrelated to Jesus, for the prologues to the Gospel of John and Hebrews connect the Son with the process by which God created the world. In his own life Jesus created a community; he demonstrated power to use the natural order as the instrument to accomplish his purposes of the heart and mind. Here is the pattern for our life, too, to utilize the creative power entrusted to us to transform the world from heartless process to a humane place where men can live together in the way that God from the beginning has intended.

The second event in the calendar is the Christmas season, beginning ever earlier in the fall and becoming increasingly secular in its character. Because Christmas is part of the rhythm of our life, our chief responsibility in the church is to shape the celebrations of this season so that its meaning can be transmitted. The season then will reinforce Christian faith and incorporate Christians more firmly into the church. The Advent-Christmas-Epiphany cycle, as celebrated in the church, should emphasize the joy of our faith, the sense of peace and calm that are associated with Jesus' birth, and contrast sharply with the frantic pressure of secular observances of this season. The recovery of family celebrations, such as the lighting of the Advent candles in homes, might be included in this dimension of the Christian observance of the season. The church's total program of Christmas activities, furthermore, should be religious, leaving the merrymaking, which is in itself good but largely irrelevant to the church's purpose, to organizations with no responsibility for instilling faith. The liturgical life of a congregation should be designed to make full use of the season's possibilities—with churches carefully decorated, lighting wisely done, and services adapted to the themes of this season. All that is said and done can thus write on the hearts and minds of people the mystery of our faith—that in the fullness of time God came to dwell among us.

The celebration of Easter is more difficult these days because here is focused the contest between new mood and old form. The very cause of rejoicing that made Easter the major festival of the Christian year is now a cause of growing intellectual difficulty. Death is less real to people now than it once was. We see so little of it, especially during childhood and the early adult years. In the city instead of on the

109

farm, we no longer watch animals portray before our eyes the cycle of birth, maturation, old age, and death. People live longer than once was the case, and it is now possible to look forward to the full life cycle. Yet death is more real than it once was. The logistics of putting all the population of the world from all the history of man in some one place, even a spiritual one, are staggering. There is a growing readiness to talk about the meaning of life and death within the context of this immediate realm of experience. The imagery of biblical speech with respect to death is less helpful than once it was. More and more people are like the officer of a church who told me, after I had spoken to a group on this theme, that we have to find a way of telling Mrs. Jones that when she dies she is dead and that meaning in her life must be found in the face of this fact.

Three consequences for liturgical practice follow. The first is that Christmas will become the major day and Easter the secondary. In one sense the meaning of Christmas is just as much cast in the language of myth as is the meaning of Easter. God's descent to earth, the meaning of the one holy day, is as non-historical as is Jesus' ascent to heaven. Yet the religious imagery surrounding the birth of a child comes close to the native sense of human life. We can speak of divinity and humanity in the same breath when we see Jesus, because we tend to speak those same

110

words when we see any newborn infant. There is no other way of affirming the promise that a child brings into the world. The whole life of man responds joyfully, expectantly, tenderly to the historical event and the church's testimony to its meaning. With Easter there is greater difficulty. Death we understand; resurrection stories strain our ability to comprehend. The interpretation of faith is further removed from the totality of our experience as human beings.

A second consequence is that the season of Lent will become more prominent than it has been in the past. The tragic vision of life is very much a part of our sensibilities—we see it played out in the sacrifices that ordinary people make for the causes in which they believe. We see how people are crushed by life and yet die ennobled. This same depiction of meaning is present in the passion narratives telling of Jesus' last days. With that man we can identify as he faces perplexing decisions, as he struggles against the fear of death, as he flinches from the awesomeness of his lonely mission. Easy as it is to make Lent into a season of moral exhortation, church leaders must avoid this temptation and instead concentrate upon the representative story and its counterparts in the life of man today. Then Lent will become a carrier of the gospel.

A third consequence is that new imagery will

emerge that helps people today internalize portions, at least, of the Easter story. An example is the palm tree, which Susanne Langer suggests as a figure of speech for the life of the human race and of each man within it. This tropical plant is made up of a long, slender trunk topped by fronds, more like a fern than a tree. When one frond matures and falls, it leaves its stub, which becomes part of the trunk of the tree. Through the years the palm tree grows by the gradual building up of these stubs of the fronds. The life of man is composed from the imperceptible stubs of human life—the enduring remainders of what one has been. Life with its varied splendors is that time when the frond is full and waves in the wind. Then comes death, and the frond falls to the earth and disappears; but there remains in the tree of man something of that frond, that life, and the tree grows. So it was with Jesus of Nazareth, whose death and resurrection proclaim this faith in cosmic dimension. So it is, we believe, with all of us.

This provisional design, with its tentativeness with respect to truth and the patterns of life, will not recover for the churches that swelling support which filled them to overflowing in the decade following the close of World War II. Never again will we live in that kind of world—we know too much about the universe; we know too little about ourselves. The new styles of personal life are far advanced, and we must live with this new way of organizing time and energy. What I have proposed is a way of maintaining significant contact with people who will not be in church on every Sunday. It concentrates the church's whole life upon those forms of "ritual becoming high art" which most effectively bear the gospel and incorporate people into the Christian vision of life.

How Do We
Get There from Here?

The liturgical style and practice that I have been describing do not prevail at the present time. In some churches the service is bland, in others confused and uncertain, in others stiffened by archaic forms and words. The style and content of congregational life are the result of the confident and expansionist mood that characterized the postwar years when churches grew regardless of what was done in them. The changes that I am proposing are efforts to develop ecclesiastical life for the era that began in the late

fifties when religion passed crest. The questions that
we face are these: Can this change in style and practice be achieved? Is it worth the effort?

During my first years of seminary teaching I urged
students to move in this new direction and suggested
to them how this movement might be carried out.
One reason for my returning to a congregation
during my first sabbatical leave was to find out in
actual practice whether what I had been saying
proved out. In Seattle I confronted an aging congregation of fifteen hundred members, mainly white and
middle-class. The staff was well prepared and effective
in the various areas of their major responsibilities,
but as is generally the case in Protestant churches
they had had only meager formal training in the
history and theology of worship, and their various
pastoral responsibilities had not required them to keep
abreast of current developments in this field. The
Sunday service when I arrived was in good taste; its
tone was serious and the preaching strong. Since they
were a congregation of the Christian Church (Disciples of Christ), their regular Sunday service included sermon and communion. Yet it departed far
from the classical norms as has been done in many
Disciple churches—introduction of adoration, responsive reading of Scripture, anthem, pastoral
prayer, communion meditation and prayer, distribu-
tion of communion, offering, doxology, sermon, in-

vitation hymn. Staff and other leaders indicated a readiness to rearrange the service on special occasions but felt little of my urgency about change. It was clear that revisions could be achieved, but the question had to be faced: What difference will it make? Early in October we modified the regular order for use on a festival Sunday when people were resigned to experimentation. They were happy enough the next Sunday to return to the familiar form.

I was then taken out of the city for a time, and on one Sunday in my travels visited two churches. One service and sermon dealt directly with the nature of contemporary life and Christian responsibility in this world. The other spoke about inner contentment, showing no awareness of the anguish of public life in America during this decade of violent passage. In one church it was evident that the long hot summer just concluded required the rearranging of the structures of the church and world. In the other church it was as though the long hot summer had not been burning at all. In the one church the order of worship came close to what I had been advocating; in the other the conventional Disciple order still held out. I would be naïve if I were to assume that shifting around the order of worship would effect renewal, for such work might be but an exercise in self-deception. What had to be involved was more than tinkering with words and ceremonies; it was the creation of a liturgical style and practice that were suited to this time of upheaval. Much besides the Sunday service would have to be dealt with—the style and form of congregational life, the deployment of money, the forms of metropolitan mission, the reformulation of theology, the recovery of genuine forms of diocesan life. But my presumed expertise, and thus my major responsibility, was the church's liturgy. I returned to Seattle convinced that to the degree that liturgical reform represents response to the crisis of our time it is worth all the effort we can give it. The pace of experimentation and education while I was with my church had to be stepped up. My colleagues on the church staff were willing to follow my lead.

The revisions on the October Sunday had not been satisfactory, for in trying to retain the emotional tone and the details of the regular service, we had not sufficiently strengthened the liturgy either in its style or its form. We determined on the next experimental Sunday, the Sunday before Thanksgiving, to reform more drastically. We rearranged the service so that it moved according to the classical sequence. By stripping away unnecessary devotional elements, especially extra prayers, we simplified it. The communion prayer was strengthened by a dialogue sung by choir and congregation, thus augmenting the usually skimpy prayer given by a nonprofessional minister. We heightened the dramatic character of the service by using trumpets and vigorous choral music, which incorporated both choir and congregation in an eloquent recital of Christian faith. On the Sunday before Christmas a similar approach was taken to liturgical revision. By that time leaders of the congregation were prepared to discuss more seriously the relationship of liturgical style to congregational life. Previously, the discussions had been largely academic but now they had become intensely personal. We could tell, however, that one practical factor still clouded judgment. Occasional festival Sundays had problems: normal processes such as the movement of ushers and servers had to be rearranged; the reflexive anticipations of the congregation were bound to the ordinary service, and there was a feeling of strangeness to the special celebration.

The way to reduce this problem was to use the revised order for a period of several Sundays, and Lent seemed to be the right time. Drawing upon our experiences of the three previous experimental Sundays, we devised an order that seemed workable and appropriate to this particular season. Throughout the winter I had met with church groups and interpreted the meaning of worship and discussed liturgical form and style. Now further communication was undertaken in order to interpret the Lenten order to the congregation. A special sermon series was designed to fit the mood of this season, interpreting the meaning of Christ's passion. On Palm Sunday the choir sang Bach's "Christ Lay in the Bonds of Death" in place of the sermon. On Easter the same order, with appropriate changes in mood, was used. By this time we could tell that the new order worked and provided an instrument that was more flexible and yet theologically stronger than the service that it had replaced.

Plans for the Sundays after Easter had already been laid. Those Sundays, to be called "Days of Rejoicing," were to express the joys and hopes of people in the congregation. We talked with groups and individuals, asking them the causes of their fears, their hopes, their joys. How, we asked, can these qualities be expressed more fully in the acts of worship that we conduct on Sundays? And we sought to show them how traditional liturgical forms can carry the varieties of meaning that a diverse congregation brings to the service on Sundays. With slight modifications in detail, the same service that had been used during Lent was used on the "Days of Rejoicing." We introduced a contemporary reading just before the sermon—on one Sunday from Martin Luther and on another from Martin Luther King, Jr. One Sunday made use of contemporary folk music and protest songs, with guitars; and another, a musical ensemble that represented the current renaissance of interest in baroque music.

We asked people what their opinions were after these weeks of experimentation. Some did not like what had been done and urged that we go back to the way it had been at the beginning of the year, but the overwhelming response favored the new. Young people said that the sermon was easier to listen to when it came early in the hour. Someone said that the service seemed shorter (even though it took the same length of time—one hour). Another person commented on how right it was that after the sermon we meet together at communion. One officer of the church, who had been unenthusiastic about the changes when they were proposed, stated that if we were to go back the old style would be terribly tame. My own conclusion after the year's experience was that this kind of change is possible. The service that results provides a stronger and more flexible instrument for conveying the gospel and our response to it than the conventional services that prevail in Protestantism.

Yet a major change in the style and order of worship is not easily accomplished. With this fact in mind a minister in Kansas City asked me, as I recited our Seattle experiences: "You were there for a whole year; what can a church without such a staff person do?" The answer is that more important than the person is a process. Guided by principles that form that process, congregations across the country can

120

make significant progress toward liturgical renewal.

The first principle in this process is that change must be based on knowledge. We have lived through a long period when the order of worship was determined largely by the pastor on the basis of his own theories and the strength of residual congregational resistance to change. This attitude can no longer be tolerated. Because the pastor as liturgical authority represents the church as a whole and not just himself, he must listen to its voice and depart from it only when driven by conscience. The only way that he will learn about this mind of the church is by study, either in consultation with knowledgeable people or by reading reliable texts in this field. It is not enough, however, that the pastor study; his congregation must also be brought into the circle of knowledge. Over a period of time their attention can be focused on worship, in classes, by means of sermons, by written materials that are made available. Changes should be planned in good time to permit consultation with musicians and church officers who share in the making of decisions and leading of worship. This studied approach to change does much to reduce the resistance that understandably arises when people are caught off guard by changes in the form of words and actions that they associate with their time together in church.

A second principle is that significant changes in worship require vigorous leadership combined with respect for the sensitivities of the congregation. Some aspects of the church program can properly be made by members of the church without any consultation with the pastor. Other aspects of congregational life are of such a nature that only the pastor can make them. Most elements stand somewhere between these opposing ends of the continuum. Because questions about worship stand much closer to the pole of pastoral decision than of congregational decision, the pastor must move vigorously and imaginatively to put into practice the liturgical style and form that his studies have convinced him are right. Changes in the order of worship are not made by majority vote of the congregation, yet the pastor does not dare to run over the people thoughtlessly or carelessly. As much as possible their willingness to go along should be gained even if their eager support cannot be secured immediately.

The third principle is that experimentation is in order. One reason is to find the right local use. The building, musical resources, habits, and attitudes of the people make a difference in what can be staged in any given place. Even when a well-proved order of worship is used, the fine detail of performance will vary from place to place, and only experimentation can lead to the establishing of this form. Another reason is to enable the people to adjust. It takes time and experience for a congregation to come to the place that it can use the new pattern with as much satisfaction as it did the previous one. Experimentation enables the congregation to realize the vitality that is inherent in the form. Worship is high art and requires skill and insight, both of which are related to experience.

A fourth principle is that preaching must be carefully planned for the period of experimentation with new forms of worship. Because the sermon is the longest part of a service and does much to determine the tone of the entire act of worship, the minister must give very careful thought to his own homiletical style so that what he says fits. The question is not what he says so much as how he says it. His interpretation of contemporary affairs and what they demand of people must, on the one hand, be shaped by his understanding of God's way of work as it is interpreted by biblical writers. It must, on the other hand, free his hearers to confess their sin, express their thanksgiving, and renew their baptismal vows by means of the eucharistic service. Rather than being a limitation on the power of preaching, this restriction of the mood intensifies its forcefulness and gives it the greatest possible likelihood of effectiveness. The minister dare not assume that his current homiletical form is satisfactory. Too much of the time it is not.

Failure in liturgical reform is frequently the result of preaching that is out of character.

I have tried to say that the reform of liturgical style and the order of worship is both worth the effort and possible. The conclusion is that congregations must begin this process and move toward reform of the liturgy. At this point I want to speak to specific problems that will be encountered when revision is undertaken. Some of these problems will be faced by my own denomination, the Christian Church (Disciples of Christ). Disciples have one distinct advantage over most other Protestants because our liturgical tradition includes preaching and the Lord's Supper as the standard elements of the Sunday service. In nearly every one of our congregations these two elements of classical Christian worship are present. From our beginnings in the early nineteenth century we have at the same time stood in the free tradition of worship, shaped by experiences on the frontiers of western America under leadership largely self-taught in matters liturgical. Common practice was for a rural congregation to meet on Sunday for a service of songs and prayer followed by Bible study according to age groups loosely graded. Then the congregation would reassemble for communion. All this was customarily led by local leaders chosen because of their maturity of life and competence to guide the congregation. When a preacher was available, he would take over when the congregation had completed their regular service. In 1966 I preached in a church, not far from Indianapolis, that still follows this pattern.

In most Disciple congregations the customs described above have been adapted to accord with the presence of more permanent professional leadership. Sunday church school and a service with preaching and communion are distinct events. Yet habits learned long ago prevail and stand in the way of adopting the liturgical style and form that I have been describing. The luxury of deviation from the Christian consensus concerning worship has been too long enjoyed. We must now change from the practice that has been dominant for the past half-century to that which measures up to the best of contemporary standards.

It is normal among Disciples to have as presidents at communion people who have in recent years been referred to as lay elders. When the practice began these men were the only ministers we had, and they functioned at the table as ministers. The practice may have been slightly irregular, when viewed by other denominations, but at least it was well thought out and responsibly done. Through the years, however, we developed a trained and salaried ministry whose status grew while that of the elder diminished until the men who had once been our ministry were clearly considered laymen in contrast to the ordained persons who preached and delivered a communion meditation before communion began.

Our problem now is what to do. A new dimension has developed in the Consultation on Church Union, for their documents make room for ministers who do not have theological training and who receive no salary for their work. In somewhat more sophisticated theological language, these writings say much the same thing that Disciples once said about their elders. Yet Disciples are not now sure whether they want to recover the ministerial character of their eldership. Indeed, some Disciples believe that to do so would be to make a serious mistake, because the nature of contemporary society requires professional staff people for such functions as these.

Disciples have two choices. One is to move immediately toward reshaping their eldership so that these men become the kind of ministers that the Consultation on Church Union advocates. In most congregations this course of action would require a sharp reduction in the number of men who are chosen for this office. More extended preparation for functions of pastoral care and leadership than is now provided would have to be developed. We would have to revise their functions in church life so that they act more as ministers and less as conservative laymen.

The other choice is to make clear what some people

say is the case—that elders are laymen and not ministers, that their functions now are specialized roles of lay leadership rather than nonprofessional forms of pastoral leadership. This course of action would lead quickly to a reassignment of their liturgical duties. Instead of the communion prayer, they would share as worship leaders at other points in the service, and the minister would pray the major prayer at the communion table.

For some Disciples this redeployment of elders is dictated by reasons other than those of traditions concerning the ministry. When the service is arranged so that the communion prayer is the major prayer of the liturgy, it is important that the words used be the right ones. Who is sensitive enough to the conditions of the world, to the needs of the congregation, to the implications of the gospel, to frame that prayer? Who can handle himself competently enough for the strength of the prayer to be evident to the congregation? Practical experience leads some church people to conclude that very few nonprofessional leaders combine these qualities. The tendency, therefore, is to move the traditional Disciple elder away from the table for these liturgical reasons regardless of what theology and church order may permit or require.

Although I still am reluctant to take sides in this question, my experience this year with one church, in addition to my observances in many places, forces me to the dual conviction that the communion prayer must be strengthened and that in most cases this means the restricting of the number of persons who are permitted to lead the congregation at this point.

I must speak to other Protestants who share with Disciples a heritage in the free tradition, whose spiritual formation has been on the frontier as has been ours. My impression is that their normal practice is far removed from the liturgical style that I am advocating and that they, too, must now begin seriously to change the way of liturgical life in their congregations. The crucial question for them, of course, is how vigorously to move toward the recovery of the full service of Word and Sacrament as the standard Sunday act of worship. The problem is intensified because for many of them the normal Sunday service is clearly in the free tradition, emphasizing extemporaneous prayer, extensive variety, and freedom from fixed forms. Yet their custom requires that when communion is celebrated they make use of the prescribed text with fixed wording, archaic and heavy style, and ponderous tone. The contrast is too much to bear, and their people reject the sacramental. Their pastors refuse this retreat from the prophetic and open character of the preaching service to the priestly and restricted character of the sacramental ritual.

For some of them the problem has been reduced

by recent revisions of official liturgical documents. They now provide, as they did not previously do, a flexibility and modernity that come close to matching the style that has long been used in Sunday services in some of these churches. For these the possibility of decision is clear. By wise pastoral leadership, by careful experimentation, by judicious instruction of their people they can move toward the full service of Word and Sacrament rather quickly. An interim step is to follow the counsel in recently published liturgies that the first part of the service of Word and Sacrament be used as the regular service even when there is no communion. By concluding each Sunday with offering and prayers much of the character of the full service is maintained.

Even the churches with archaic, prescribed liturgies can move in this direction. When it is necessary to use a free and contemporary form of worship, it could be a partial service of Word and Sacrament in the style and form that I have suggested. When the time for union of our separated churches comes, in the near future let us pray, then these churches could move toward even fuller use of contemporary forms.

Throughout these pages I have talked about worship while giving no attention to other aspects of church life and program. At some time the question has to arise as to the relationship between worship and program. What kind of church is presupposed by this talk of a new style of worship? Is it possible for such a church to survive in the time when we are going through such revolutions in the nature of institutional life? If it does, if this new style of worship is established, will it save the nation? Can the smoke of city fires be quenched by this kind of ecclesiastical life? To these questions we must now turn.

Can Such a Church Survive?

In contemporary American life there are three recognizable types of church. Evangelical Protestantism is a continuation into our time of theology, personal life style, and congregational life that were dominant a half-century ago. It uses biblical language easily, resists the development of theological discourse cast in other intellectual idioms (such as philosophy or sociology), and builds certainty of faith upon vivid and warm personal religious experience. Liberal Protestantism is a continuation into our time of the theology, personal life style, and congregational life that during past decades have combined to make the one significant alternative to evangelical Protestantism. In its commitment to communication with modern man, it has used various styles of language—philosophical, psychological, sociological—often to the virtual exclusion of biblical and traditional theological discourse. Its desire has been to meet contemporary needs effectively, and it has utilized worship and congregational program to accomplish this purpose.

A third type of Protestantism, difficult to name because its character is just now becoming evident, is more determined than has been liberal Protestantism to represent the major tradition of Christianity and is more committed than evangelical Protestantism to communicate with people who have lost contact with the Bible, traditional theology, and clearly recognized religious experience. This third type is trying to unite the catholic-reformed-evangelical streams of classical Christian tradition. It has a tough-mindedness about the needs of contemporary life, dealing rigorously and often unconventionally with questions of faith and ethics.

I grew up in an evangelical church from which I received the Christian faith, a gift for which I am ever grateful. Indeed, churches of this type continue to engender faith in large numbers of people. Their members stay close to biblical categories of life and thought, see a sharp contrast between church and world, and struggle incessantly to create from within the church's life structures that can take over the whole world of honorable human endeavor. These churches have the kind of protective spiritual climate that enables people within them to come to strong personal faith and practice before being subjected to the confusions of public life. Yet I can no longer participate in this kind of church, for I cannot accept the version of the Christian faith that it represents or the tendency to define the Christian life by specific laws inflexibly maintained. I cannot accept the view that God's purpose is to bring social structures into the institutional control of the church, and I cannot accept the retreat from public faith to private piety that so often develops among people in this type of church.

While liberal Protestantism is less effective than evangelical Protestantism in transmitting the faith to the new generation, this kind of church is able to preserve the faith for some people who might otherwise leave it. The tentativeness of viewpoint, the provisional attitude toward faith and practice, the willingness to advance by stages appeal to people who find themselves unable to continue in churches of the first type. Commendable, too, is the concern sometimes demonstrated for work within the institutions of society in order to lead toward the humanizing of them. Yet I can no longer agree that this kind of church is the one that we should try to develop. Tentativeness too easily leads to complete indecision or lack of strength. Churches of this type easily succumb to the temptation to conform to folkways and customs, right or wrong. Religion too easily becomes a way of justifying the existing order rather than a way of improving it. As important as the emphasis upon inner strength may be, it can become a means of self-justification instead of the means of rising above obstacles that confront men.

The third style of Protestantism interests me because it is the one form of Protestant Christianity that I believe will continue to be a living option for people in the generation ahead and capable of making a difference in future American society. It will for a long time be smaller than the other two types; it will continue to search for the right way of life to recommend to people. This third type may be able to engender the faith in the lives of people who have not previously been a part of the Christian community, and in this sense it is like churches of the first type. Yet the way that the faith is engendered, and the qualities of that faith, will be quite different. Like churches of the second type it will be able to sustain that faith during later years because of its intellectual realism and serious demands. People touched by its life will become leaders in the humanizing of society and the creation of a new humanity, which is God's intention for the life of the world.

The style of worship that I have described fits churches of this third style. The possibilities for that kind of liturgical life and the prospects for this new style of Protestantism go hand in hand. The one question is whether such churches can survive.

There are laymen in large numbers who want this kind of church. Because of a native streak of seriousness in their makeup or some powerful experience that has moved them in this direction they are determined that their churches should be the kind that can move human life and society toward higher goals. There are many ministers who want this kind of church, too. Some have left conventional ministries because they have not been able to develop such a church; others continue to work toward the creation of congregations that represent this third style.

The evidence, however, indicates that a great many church people do not want a church marked by the style that I have described. Although one reads of churches that move in this direction—in Cleveland and Cincinnati, in Washington and Philadelphia— one also reads of churches that have broken apart in the effort to find renewal. Most ministers understand the pastor of one large church in Oklahoma whom I heard attacked by younger men impatient for change: "You have to give ministers of churches like mine time. We have to carry this whole thing along, and that is hard to do." He told of his own witness in his congregation to open housing covenants and of the serious decline in attendance, which he attributed to that kind of courageous leadership. It is hard to bring about the change—hard because some church people will resist any change, hard because some members are in church only to be entertained or cured or flattered. Change is hard to bring about because some ministers are too abrasive or not abrasive enough, because some insist too much upon their version of the gospel or because they have lost their faith entirely. But the problems are deeper than these.

One more significant factor inhibiting the growth of these churches is the nature of human behavior. In the Old Testament the weak and faltering ones numbered more than the prophets. Most of the people who left Egypt under Moses worshiped the golden calf in the wilderness and yearned for food back in Egypt's slavery. The judges of Israel and the prophets who followed them generations later faced the defection of the masses. Indeed, history is the story of this division of man into the few with vision and responsibility and the many with feeble will and private occupations. This fact still holds true. If the many are to be in church at all, it will be because they are coaxed and wheedled, entertained and healed.

Ministers whose program recognizes this fact and builds upon it will continue in the immediate future to preside over sizable congregations. If they are fortunate enough to possess personal charm and intellectual strength, too, their chance of success is even greater.

Ministers in churches of the third kind, however, tend to be restrained. Some of them, unable to bring themselves to work the gimmicks, want "class" to be their sole attraction, liturgical style and homiletical strength their only methods. This purity of motive and style runs a poor second to the flamboyance and methodology of those whose stance toward institutional life is geared to a pragmatic assessment of human nature. The problem is compounded by the fact that people who are most likely to be attracted to this third kind of church resist the opportunity to become involved. Some have become disenchanted with the other kinds of Protestantism, seeing one kind as an anachronism hanging over from an earlier age when man knew less than he now does, and seeing the other as too bland to make any real difference. Having abandoned the currently dominant alternatives, they do not easily come within reach of a third possibility. Furthermore, many of these people have developed substitutes for religion and see no reason to change. Many do not know what the third style has to offer. Even when they do know, most are not willing to engage in conventional church programming. Thus, any person or congregation setting out to develop this third style is facing the possibility of severe institutional pressures.

A second significant factor is that church institutions, long overextended, are now facing the likelihood of cutbacks to a more reasonable level. Denominational judicatories have greatly expanded their staffs, frequently in a time when their constitutencies have begun to decline. Congregations have large physical plants, much of it used but a few hours a week. Their organizational structure is complex, their decision-making apparatus unwieldy, their institutional life diverse and time-consuming. What is happening now is that this postwar institutional expansion is going sour. Attitudes toward volunteer organizations are more caustic than once was the case. People are more selective with their benevolences, whether of time or money. Once again, the very people who are likely to be attracted to the third style of church are the very ones most affected by this disenchantment with institutions.

A third factor is that all the churches, regardless of their style, are dealing with a smaller proportion of the populace. The Christian faith may be as logically possible as it ever was, but psychologically it is less viable than formerly was the case. The mood of our time conditions daily life, and no amount of reasoning or practical activity will make it go away. Our children will be affected by it, some more so than by the liturgical point of view that surrounds them in the church. When they reach maturity some of them will continue within the church, and some will drift away. Inspiration for art, literature, music, political life, and social standards will come from diversified and often conflicting sources. Christian domination of the life of man has come to an end, and this vision of life must now make room for others that seek men's loyalties. It does no good to deplore this development or to oppose it, for a homogeneous society cannot be maintained. This the Puritan settlers discovered in seventeenth-century New England, and the lesson has been repeated in various experiments since then. Moreover, this pluralism is one of the sources of great excitement in our world, for the influx of new ideas and thought structures, new forms of music and art, additional visions of life and how it should be lived, has created an epoch bursting with promise.

We must be candid. Churches today are strong when several factors come together—vigorous and able ministers, favorable location and external circumstances, theological and programmatic emphases that do not threaten existing social structures and personal styles of life. Churches of the first and second types tend to fall into this pattern, but the kind of church I am advocating does not. Can it survive when it has an able and vigorous ministry, and perhaps favorable external circumstances, but at the same time questions the existing social structures and refuses to cater to the private and personal interests that have so dominated church program in recent decades?

Some people answer no, claiming that the institutional objectives in the third style churches are too utopian, that there are not enough people or enough money to keep the bills paid, especially since they are contracted to keep up institutional structures inherited from previous times. Occasional examples might survive, but their numbers would be small and their influence upon society limited—if for no other reason, because their coverage is so slight. Some who say "no" turn their answer into a cause of rejoicing. The faith will survive, they believe, with only the slightest outward institutional evidence. Freed from the alien forms of great institutions, the faith will now be able to move into the bloodstream of modern life, bringing health to all dimensions of society. Others who say "no" find only cause for despair. Because they believe that institutions, corporate entities, are the units that make up society, the loss of public and powerful churches means the virtual loss to modern life of the faith itself.

A second answer is that vigorous churches of this

new type can survive but that they will be small, trim societies of the elite. The rank and file, the masses, will continue to be in the churches that cater to their interests and support what they already find valuable in their current life styles. Some who hold this point of view are quite willing that the two orders of ecclesiastical life continue. The large churches provide money and a source of manpower, while the small, elite churches provide the application of the gospel that really counts. The conclusion some make enthusiastically is that so long as each kind of church fulfills its congenial mission, the total effect is satisfactory. Some who give this second answer do so with little enthusiasm. They question one another's motives; they may even impugn the validity of the other's work.

A third answer is yes, but only if these churches are mixed creations. Here is where I want to stand, and to do so requires that I explain my position with some care. What one political writer said of an audience that faced Nelson Rockefeller at a county fair is true for a great part of our citizenry: "For this was a Lawrence Welk crowd, at ease with home permanents, pickup trucks, county fairs, and—one suspected—Barry Goldwater." When Rockefeller spoke to them of urban rot he might as well have been using Swahili. Common stock American society deals with the daily necessities of life, makes a living, rears a family; it is an easy-going and conservative majority of the human race. Although there are variations in their urbanity, the majority of our people are far behind the pacesetters, whether it be in clothing fashions or modern music or the life of the spirit. I want a church of the new style to be so conceived that it can encompass within its "catholicity" a great many common stock Americans, even though these very people will always be some distance removed from the pacesetters.

Some pastors are so constituted that they cannot stop for the followers but must stay out ahead with the advance scouts. Most of us, however, will do our exploring from within the main company, which includes father and mother, friend and co-worker in the long life that God grants us. Because they are people with needs as well as responsibilities, we must care for them. From its ranks, furthermore, rise up leaders of the new elite who through the processes of institutional life and program are helped along to become the effective people they potentially are. The ideas and styles advocated by the leaders may be wrong, or their methods unproductive; while contact with the common stock is sometimes stultifying, it can also be life-giving by correcting excesses and giving human substance to intellectual ideals.

The combining of this catholicity of humanity and the new style of church life bears implications for the Sunday service, for church program, for attributes of leaders, and for the processes of decision. The Sunday service must at the same time be the spiritual home for the total membership and a symbol of the new style of congregational life. If this cannot be achieved, then there is no hope of maintaining the mixed church, for whichever quality wins, crowding out the other, will in time determine what kind of church is going to exist in that place. In a mixed congregation the new style must establish the tone and point the direction of advance. Yet it must do so in such a way as to utilize folkways that represent catholicity, for they are the conveyer, the means of communication that bring the people toward the new style. Two words of counsel are needed, however. The folkways themselves represent various standards and a church interested in the new style must always insist that only those of highest standard be used in worship. Second, the expressions of the new style must be carried out so as to avoid the critical and condescending tone that so often creeps in as people move beyond the commonly accepted folkways.

In some parts of the congregation's program the new style must be expressed with no modification. Special educational opportunities and projects designed for local mission must be developed in order to assist people of the church to learn how to represent the gospel fully in the structures of personal and public affairs. Unfortunately, a great part of the congregation will not participate in such affairs, for they never are jarred out of their own sphere of private interests. But the leaders of a church must continue their labors with those who will listen and respond, taking heart as the number gradually grows.

At the same time, catholicity must be acknowledged by pastoral gentleness toward those who resist change and by sensible utilization of the dynamics of institutional vitality. Family harmony and vitality require a certain amount of attention to those very qualities. Some activities have to be undertaken solely because to do so adds interest and excitement to the lives that people live together. Even more so is this deliberate attention to institutional vitality needed when the social organism is something as complex and ponderous as a volunteer society. Processes of communication and troubleshooting, of variation and reassurance, of adopting goals and moving toward them must be undertaken because that is the nature of institutions. The danger always is that institutional vitality becomes the objective rather than a means to a higher goal. I do not know any way of guaranteeing that this transposition of goals will not take place. Yet I am convinced that the risk must be taken, for the unwillingness to pay attention to institutional vitality is a sure way of lowering the chances of survival for such churches.

In order to carry on this kind of church program a special kind of minister is needed. He must have a clear view of the gospel and the facts of contemporary life, be sensitive to the fears, sins, and loves of his people, be able to pace himself and his ministry, always moving toward further goals, yet never moving faster than circumstances permit. Perhaps most important, he must see himself with a high degree of realism, for ministers, as much as anyone else, can misunderstand themselves and misjudge their own motivations and methods. There are times when the failure of program in the new style is due less to the inherent difficulties in that kind of program than to the misdirected zeal or mistaken judgment of pastoral leaders.

A special combination of minister and people is also important. He cannot hope that his people will agree with his every view or that they will be able to support every venture that he recommends. They can easily become his opponents, just as he may become their antagonist. The question that must be faced is whether it is possible for churches to have lay officers who are willing to let pastoral leaders move to develop a program that far exceeds their own views and wishes. Can officers who represent conservative social and economic views permit their minister to advocate from pulpit and in city life what seem like radical views and policies? Can they know that their church is associated in the public mind with their minister's new-style policies and yet support its program and maintain its institutional strength?

This kind of arrangement does in some places exist, and certain qualities seem to be present when it does: the ability of minister and people to talk openly about their differences, yet in such a way as to maintain the sense of the other's integrity; an ability to find common ground in Christian faith that is even more fundamental than the sharply divergent views of social policy; a serious effort to meet one another so as to move toward understanding the motivations of the other; a profound respect on the part of laymen for the minister's professional standing and competence; a profound respect on the part of the minister for the complexity of the issues facing his people. Perhaps more important than all these factors is the recognition in the public life of the church, especially in its policy-making bodies, that this divergence not only exists but is to be expected and desired.

This attitude places a great burden upon the minister. From his people he receives a great trust, and his temptation will be to abuse it by impetuous speech and action and by unreasonable insistence that all reasonable men agree with him. This attitude also places burdens upon the laymen, for their temptation is to fall back when the pastor's position hurts them individually as it is bound to do on some occasions.

They then seek to force him out by coercion, withdrawing funds and creating unrest behind the scenes.

A third requirement is that the bishop be sympathetic to the development of new-style churches. A man whose chief aim is the preservation of the existing institutional strength will value peace above all else. His temptation is to remove the irritant, which ordinarily will be the minister who runs counter to the prevailing prejudices and self-interests of the congregation. What the bishop ought to do instead is to make ready for tension. Before a minister is assigned the bishop must speak seriously to the officers of a congregation, instructing them to expect tension because the minister has been trained to lead in such a way that tension is bound to result and because he, the bishop, expects his ministers to be in the advance guard. The bishop should help church officers to develop attitudes and structures that enable this creative tension to exist so that it results in increased institutional vitality rather than in the destruction of the church. He should counsel them on how to counteract militant minorities within the congregation who may resist both the minister and the solid institutional support given him by leaders of the church, many of whom do not agree with him. The bishop must be willing to enter into church disputes that may arise and work toward resolution of the issues instead of removal of the irritant. He must develop flexibility of procedure rather than operate on pragmatic rules of thumb about sizes of the minority and possible institutional outcomes. The bishop must deal with his pastors, goading some of them to more vigorous witness and curbing the impetuousness and poor sense of others. The result could be a high level of tolerance, an ability to live with extended differences of theology, life-style, and involvement in mission. When these conditions develop, the possibility of a new-style church surviving is quite good.

I fear, however, that these conditions do not now exist in the great numbers that we need. Too long has there been a tradition of government by intimidation or manipulation, of problem-solving by cowardly action instead of resolute facing of issues, of ambiguity and double speech by ministers, of local empire-building by laymen, of failure to deal openly with the grave issues of society. We now face the consequences of institutional life that has depended upon superficial goodwill rather than solid processes that distribute responsibility and provide for decision-making that is honorable and effective.

Even when the seminaries can prepare a minister to work in these conditions, and this is in itself hard enough to do, there still is the tradition of official boards who rule by intimidation. There still is the vast ecclesiological bureaucracy that promotes the unprincipled but efficient organization man and penalizes the abrasive innovator who so desperately needs support and guidance in the midst of the crises that he helps to create. I wish that my year in close contact with the churches could have renewed my confidence in prospects for the future. I have met ministers and laymen who yearn for churches of the new style, who work toward their realization, who even now are giving themselves to the kind of Christian witness that the current crisis demands.

But there are so few.

An Interesting Thought, but Can It Cool the Summer?

The survival of the church in any form is of secondary importance. The urgent matter is the survival of the nation and of the world, and here people within the religious communion hold contrasting views. In sermons during the winter of 1968, dealing with the holocaust of the 1940's when "six million of our brothers were systematically and brutally murdered," a Seattle rabbi concluded: "It is prudent to make provision for the survival of Judaism even if the worst happens." The worst, as he saw it, was the destruction of the northern hemisphere by nuclear war, the loss of all Jewry in the United States, Russia, and Israel. The prudent action that he recommended was the preservation of Jewish life and culture elsewhere, and to that end he invited his congregation to contribute to the "Fund for Australian Judaism."

A contrasting sermon was preached that winter by

a Protestant pastor of the same city, asserting that our allegiance cannot be to any separatist tradition, that instead we must be committed "to the Tradition behind and within the movements of history that liberates, unifies and reconciles the whole life of mankind." His conclusion was that once we know ourselves to be caught up in the mainstream of that Tradition, "carried along toward a future that is greater and better than any past men have known," we can be free to enter into the new forms of life that are emerging in the upheavals of our time, rejoicing in the time to come.

It may be that neither sermon is representative of the larger constituencies in which these preachers stand. One may feel deeply the anguish of genocide while the other has been spared any need of such melancholy broodings. However that may be, these two moods are widespread throughout the land. One combines prudence with doleful views, seeking practical measures to preserve the treasures of the past through the fires of the coming age, hoping for the survival of a remnant even though the whole world burns. The other view combines a measured recklessness with visionary expectation, giving full strength to the creation of a new human culture that will embrace mankind as fully as scientific civilization already does. Clustered around each of these views are others, ranging from suicidal despair to illusions of the future that stand outside any possibility of fulfillment. But these two views—prudence prompted by doubt and venturesomeness prompted by faith— are the two that most stimulate support. Around them gather the forces of revolution and reform, preservation and reaction. The dynamics of contemporary American society are revealed in these two views.

How can we choose between them? Neither one is self-evident; in opposition to each of them are evidences of major consequence, and yet some people have chosen. Among them was Martin Luther King, Jr., whose reflections after the Montgomery bus boycott suggest the set of mind that makes his kind of venturesomeness possible. Why did the Negro revolution of our time begin in Montgomery, he asked. In his answer he set aside the explanations that first came to mind. The oppressions suffered by Negroes and the emergence of a new legal structure and social climate helped to explain why there was a revolution at all but not why it began in Montgomery. The specific record of injustice in that city, the character of leaders there, the coming of new circumstances could not explain it. Every rational explanation breaks down, King said, leaving only "a divine dimension." He didn't care what name that quality was given, whether a principle of concretion, a process of integration, Being-itself, God. "Whatever the name, some extra-human force labors to create a harmony out of the discords of the universe." King's conclusion was that God had chosen Montgomery, the cradle of the Confederacy, the symbol of the Old South, to be "the proving ground for the struggle and triumph of freedom and justice in America." At the time of his death King was speaking in a similar vein. No longer did he fear death, for like Moses he had stood on the mountain and seen the promised land, the land toward which his people and all men were marching.

Neither in Montgomery nor Memphis was King prepared to let God create the millennium unaided. In those cities, and in every place where he saw this working of God, King was laboring aggressively and skillfully to organize and deploy the personal and institutional forces that were available. Major realignment of the social structures of contemporary America was the specific objective of the civil rights movement. The effective changing of those human structures, in response to the efforts of people like himself, was evidence to him that the God of history continues to work now.

King and the movement he led dramatically portray our mythic inheritance revivified. The immediate result has been not tranquillity but a surge of turmoil, sometimes undisciplined and destructive, which is the occasion for great hope for the future of society. We now see the blossoming of the great powers of mind and spirit that God has given the colored races, and white society is receiving new spiritual energies as the result. At least some of the blight upon America's life that our form of segregation has spawned is being healed. The social order still is deeply troubled, but men of faith now see evidence that God broods over the troubled land and is bringing a new cosmos out of the chaos that we have made.

We know that violence will continue, that windows will be broken again, that riots will burn down the schools our children attend, for the nation is too ponderous to be transformed instantaneously. The frustrations compounded for generations are too massive, their destructive effects upon human personality too total, their institutional forms too solid to give way without struggle. Christians who adore the Lord of history know that the struggle we now are enduring means death—to the evil and limiting forms of life that have been dominant until now. We know, too, that our current distress means the birth of that form of the human community which God intends to be the next phase of our race's life together. We therefore can live in these turbulent times with hope and confidence. In our churches week by week our vision is renewed when we hear God's word and stand as friends at his table.

There is so much yet to be done, for our problems and the current crisis are deepening. The levels of pollution grow; the ghettos expand; hunger covers more of the earth; nuclear potential spreads; fear and frustration increase. It is clear that radical social change is necessary if the new age is to come: major revision of school boundaries, moving away from strict neighborhood allocations to systems that do away with de facto segregation and the consequent narrowing of educational opportunity for the entire school population; extensive revision of tax laws and welfare systems to distribute national wealth more equitably; social integration that preserves profound cultural differences but permits complete freedom of movement and prohibits artificial restraint; the devising of new structures for securing political power and governing metropolitan areas; the removal of the lingering vestiges of the one-time Protestant domination of public schools and small-town establishments.

Yet there are so many signs of promise: the new manhood of the black peoples of this nation; the signs of spring after the long winter in the Old South; the flowering of music and architecture, of painting and urban design; the brilliance of theoretical scholarship in the arts and sciences across the nation; the militancy of social idealism in our decade; the new spirit of impatience and hope in our young; the new pluralism, which is breaking down the ancient synthesis that has grown moribund; the powerful movements in Catholic and Protestant Christianity leading toward renewal and reunion; clergy and laity who see with clear vision the depth of our crisis and who sense the possibilities within the Christian community, who seek new ways of pouring into the structure of society the moral power and spiritual vision that will lead to the coming to life of a new creation.

I return to the seminary more radical than when I left a year ago, more impatient with the sluggishness of the church and the faint heartedness of some of its clergy than I was, more fearful for the life of our nation in the immediate future, and more hopeful for the new world to come. At times, when by myself and afraid, I pray with Augustine, who in his time feared that what proved to be birth pangs were the throes of death: O God, free this city which is surrounded by the enemy; if something else seems better to you make me strong to endure your will; or at least take me out of this world unto yourself. But then I join the people of God and by the liturgy am led to see the new city that is coming down from the hand of God. With his people in all times and places I cry out:

> Holy, holy, holy, Lord God of hosts;
> Heaven and earth are full of your glory;
> Glory be to you, O Lord most high. Amen.

Appendix

Prayers for the Service

The preparation of prayers for use in public worship is a task that requires three conditions—time, sensitivity, and skill with words. Well in advance of the service that he will lead, the minister will reflect upon the service and the circumstances that give it character. Who will be present, and what qualities of heart and mind will they bring? What has gone on in the world that all people share? What influence will his sermon and the readings have upon the aim of the service? The leader must choose from these reflections the themes that most represent the congregation's intentions when the service takes place.

These he must then put into words that are brief and simple, direct and forceful, graceful but general enough that they can be used by the congregation as a whole. He will write down possible clauses or sentences, for the process of composition is one of the most important ways by which he can achieve these qualities which should mark the prayer that he presents as his congregation's approach to God.

There are, of course, occasions that do not permit this advanced preparation, when impromptu prayers are called for. Circumstances of unusual distress or suddenness demand the kind of prayer that is more a cry of deep emotion than an ordered coming before God. Even then habits learned through the careful writing of prayers will shape the movement of thought and the form of words that make up the prayers that are uttered spontaneously.

The prayers that follow are examples of those which might be used in liturgies of our time conducted according to the principles of the free tradition. Although they draw heavily upon the language of Scripture, as have the classical liturgies, each of them is a new composition prepared with specific services of worship in mind.

A. PRAYERS AT THE OFFERTORY WHEN COMMUNION DOES NOT FOLLOW

The Dialogue
  Minister: The Lord be with you.
  People: **And with your spirit.**

Minister: Lift up your hearts.
People: **We lift them to the Lord.**
Minister: Let us give thanks to the Lord our God.
People: **It is truly right so to do.**

Then the minister shall continue:

Our Father, always and everywhere we give thanks to you for your goodness and greatness. You made the sky, filling it with sun and moon and stars for us to admire. You made the earth, filling it with trees and mountains and animals for us to enjoy. You made us, filling us with dreams and powers to use everything else in your whole creation. To you be glory and praise.

Yet from the beginning we have wasted your gifts, and the world groans in pain. Therefore you came to live among us and in Jesus showed us how life should be. For this greatest gift of all we now praise you. By his death and resurrection, which we here remember, you have made possible a new life for us despite our sin.

O God, accept these prayers and acts of thanksgiving that we bring to you. Our whole selves are what we return penitently and lovingly. Come to us with the help we need. Make us what we can be. Strengthen us every day of our lives until that time when all things are made perfect by your power.

Or this:

Heaven and earth are full of your glory, O God of the ages. Your majesty shines in the eyes of all men. The dry land is watered and brings forth abundantly. Waste places are reclaimed, and cities appear so that the life of man can flourish. The eyes of the blind are opened, and those who are maimed find new life. Joy and gladness drive away sorrow and sighing. Heaven and earth are full of your glory, O God of the ages. Your majesty shines in the eyes of all men.

Yet the world still suffers, and its people mourn. Our work is faulty, our purposes confused. Pride and self-interest drive us toward distorted goals. The time of ever-lasting joy has not yet begun.

Therefore, help us, O God. Forgive our sin, and restore our union with you. Strengthen our weak hands, and drive out our fears. Send vision to the leaders of men and the spirit of sacrifice to all citizens. Give to all men everywhere, and especially those whose names and needs we today remember, what they must have in order to fulfill their various callings. Bring to its fulfilment the world that we long to enjoy.

In Christ Jesus, who points us to the life in which love prevails, we find our hope. Because of him we sing to you: Heaven and earth are full of your glory, O God of the ages. Your majesty shines in the eyes of all men.

Minister and people shall conclude the prayer by saying:

Our Father in heaven:
  Holy be your Name,
  Your kingdom come,
  Your will be done,
    on earth as in heaven.
  Give us today our daily bread.

Forgive us our sins,
    as we forgive those who sin against us.
Save us in the time of trial,
    and deliver us from evil.
For yours is the kingdom,
    the power and the glory forever. Amen.

B. COMMUNION PRAYERS OF THANKSGIVING AND PETITION

The Dialogue
    Minister: The Lord be with you.
    People: **And with your spirit.**
    Minister: Lift up your hearts.
    People: **We lift them to the Lord.**
    Minister: Let us give thanks to the Lord our God.
    People: **It is truly right so to do.**

Then the minister shall continue:

Through the generations, O God, you have led wanderers from desert places to cities where they might live. There they have found water to drink and food to eat and houses in which to dwell. In our time too you have brought us together in cities, satisfying the thirsty and filling the hungry with good things. For these your wonderful works we praise you, O God.

But today we cry out to you. In the cities of our land little children die for want of food, and strong men search for work. Neighborhoods decay while urban sprawl despoils the countryside. The air is filled with smoke and the hearts of men with despair. We have sinned. Because of our wickedness a fruitful land has become a salty waste. Forgive us, God of all mercy.

Lead all the peoples of the world from this wasteland that we have made. Send forth your Word and Presence that we may be healed. Give to all men everywhere, and especially those whose names and needs we today remember, what they must have in order to fulfill their various callings. Restore to all of us hope and courage. Then will we offer you sacrifices of thanksgiving and tell of your deeds in songs of joy:

Or this:

A new song we sing to you, O Lord, declaring your glory among the nations, your marvelous works among all peoples. From the time when you first created the world until now, you have been at work: upholding the cosmos and renewing its life, evolving new forms and destroying the old, raising up men and nations and judging them by your truth, sending us prophets and coming yourself to show us the way.

We tremble before you, God of justice and power. For we are but men, weak and sinful, little deserving of your steadfast love. Yet we come with our requests for ourselves and all men, and especially those whose names and needs we today remember, confident that for the sake of your Son you will hear us.

Give wisdom and courage, patience and humility, love

162

for mankind and powers for governing to leaders of cities and nations. Send love and zeal to ministers of the church, the servant life to its members. Inspire artists of every kind and teachers in every school. Support parents in their labors of love and children as they grow to maturity.

And to you, O God, we will sing our songs of praise:

Minister and people:

> Holy, holy, holy, Lord God of hosts;
> Heaven and earth are full of your glory;
> Glory be to you, O Lord most high.

The minister shall continue with the act of memorial:

We come to you, Father, in this spirit of thanksgiving, to celebrate the memory of Jesus Christ, your Son, who was made perfect through suffering.

On the night of his arrest he took bread
and, after giving thanks to you, broke it
and gave it to the disciples with the words:
"Take, eat: This is my body which is given for you."
In the same way after supper, he took the cup
and, having offered thanks to you,
he gave it to the disciples and said:
"Drink from this, all of you.
This cup is the new covenant sealed by my blood,
shed for you and for all men so that sins
  may be forgiven.
Whenever you do this, do it in remembrance of me."

The minister, or the minister and people together:

Father, receive us as guests at your table, now and forever. Show us your love and teach us humility that we may draw near to you and to each other. Look with favor on the gifts we bring—gifts of thanksgiving because you have done so much for us, of promise because you deserve all that we can ever be. By your life-giving Presence enable us to achieve the full life of work and devotion to humanity that these gifts pledge. Yours will be the glory and honor.

Or a seasonal prayer:

Advent, Christmas, Epiphany: Come to us, our Father. By your Spirit make present in our lives the light that burst upon men when Jesus was born. Give us courage and wisdom so that in our time we may repair the ruined cities and proclaim the year of your favor. Make us to shine like stars in a dark world, holding forth the word of life. As the magi brought gifts to the Christ child, O God, we bring ourselves, all that we are and can be. Use us to preach good news to the poor and release to the captives. By our efforts bring sight to the blind and liberty to the oppressed.

Yours will be the glory and honor.

Lent: Fill our lives, O God, and do your work in us. Teach us obedience so that we, like our Lord Jesus, may look to the interests of others and not merely to our own. Give us strength to endure suffering in his name and fortitude to face the threat of death because of our faithfulness to your will. Father, we give ourselves to you in gratitude for the privilege of believing in Christ and suffering in his name.

Yours will be the glory and honor.

Easter: Give us faith, our Father, that we might experience the power of Christ's resurrection and share his sufferings. Take away the anxiety that constantly threatens, and give us the peace that passes all understanding, the peace that Christ gives to those who are joined to him. We give ourselves to you, rejoicing that you have called us into the life of sacrifice. Fill us with the power of your Presence so that we may persevere until our goal is reached, the call to the life above in Christ Jesus.

Yours will be the glory and honor.

Minister and people shall conclude the prayer by saying:

> Our Father in heaven:
>> Holy be your Name,
>> Your kingdom come,
>> Your will be done,
>>> on earth as in heaven.
>> Give us today our daily bread.
>> Forgive us our sins,
>>> as we forgive those who sin against us.
>> Save us in the time of trial,
>>> and deliver us from evil.
> For yours is the kingdom,
>> the power and the glory forever. Amen.

C. LITANIES OF INTERCESSION
AND THANKSGIVING

I.

Day after day, O God, do we rejoice in you. Age to age proclaims your works and speaks of your splendor and glory. For you are kind and compassionate, slow to anger, and abounding in love.

In you, O God, do we rejoice.

In all your words are you faithful, in all your deeds loving. You support those who fall and raise up those who are bowed down.

In you, O God, do we rejoice.

In all your ways are you just, in all your deeds loving. You are close to those who call upon you and grant the desires of those who fear you.

In you, O God, do we rejoice.

In all your works are you glorious, in all your deeds loving. You make known to all men your everlasting kingdom and your rule over them from age to age.

In you, O God, do we rejoice.

Give praise to the Father Almighty,
to his Son Jesus Christ the Lord:

> **To the Spirit who dwells in our hearts**
> **both now and for ages unending. Amen.**

II.

Our fathers put their trust in you, O God, and you set them free. To you they cried and never in vain. Come

166

close to us in our distress. Do not leave us alone for there is no one else to help.

From the violence that destroys our cities and maims our people,

Save us, God.

From the despair that drives us to fury and distorts our power to create,

Save us, God.

From the contentment that blinds us to the plight of children and renders impotent our efforts to make a world for them,

Save us, God.

Then will we tell your name to our fellows and praise you where they assemble. Then will the hungry eat and have their fill. You shall reign, Lord of all nations. And we will live for you, and our children will serve you. To peoples yet unborn we shall declare: These things the Lord has done.

Amen.

III.

Do not be angry with us, O God our helper. Restore to us life that we may rejoice in you. Make the earth yield its fruit. Let justice march in front of you and peace follow in your steps.

**Show us your mercy, O Lord,
and give us your saving help.**

The earth has been polluted by the dwellers on its face, loose to laws and scorning statutes, breaking the eternal Compact. Therefore, the world languishes and withers.

Show us your mercy, O Lord,
and give us your saving help.

Gladness has gone from the earth, and pleasure is no more; cities are left desolate: their gates are battered down. Panic and pitfall and snares await the dwellers upon earth.

Show us your mercy, O Lord,
and give us your saving help.

A curse is crushing the earth, and its people suffer for their guilt. The vines are dry and merrymakers sigh. Earth reels like a drunken man. Under the weight of its wrongdoing earth falls down to rise no more.

Show us your mercy, O Lord,
and give us your saving help.

O Lord, you once favored the land and revived its fortunes. You forgave the guilt of your people and calmed the heat of your anger. Revive us now, O God our helper. Do not be angry with us forever.

Amen.

IV.

Heaven and earth are full of your glory, O God of power and majesty. Always and everywhere we rejoice in you, O God most high. In your Son Jesus Christ you give yourself to us, bestowing your grace and peace. Through the liberating and surprising power of your Holy Spirit you are doing new things among us. You have called us into a single family, sealed by one covenant and grounded in the same demand and promise. All glory be to you.

That communion which is your gift to broken humanity,

Restore to us, O God.

That holiness which marks your actions in us and among us,

Restore to us, O God.

That catholicity which manifests your sovereignty over the cosmos,

Restore to us, O God.

That apostolicity which links the church of all ages with Christ's mission from the beginning,

Restore to us, O God.

Above all, those gracious gifts of your Holy Spirit which empower the heroic obedience and witness of Christians,

Restore to us, O God.

Make all our actions, private and public, liturgical and secular, personal and political, the channels and tokens of your self-giving love. Then will the nations see the salvation that you have prepared. Then will we go in peace according to your promise.

Amen.

Bibliographical Notes

Ernst Cassirer, after a distinguished career in Germany, became a political exile, going first to Sweden and then to the United States where he completed his scholarly labors at Yale and Columbia. His intellectual interests ranged widely over the history of Western thought, from Greek metaphysics to Kant to theoretical physics, from Nicholas of Cusa to Goethe to contemporary studies in the psychology of perception. Most of his books have been translated into English. Among them are:

An Essay on Man. New Haven: Yale University Press, 1944, 1962. See esp. pp. 222-28.

Language and Myth. New York: Dover Publications, 1953.

The Logic of the Humanities. New Haven: Yale University Press, 1960. See esp. pp. 117-58.

The Myth of the State. New Haven: Yale University Press, 1946.

The Philosophy of Symbolic Forms. New Haven: Yale University Press, 1953, 1955, 1957.

Susanne K. Langer (1895——) has for nearly half a century been one of America's most articulate philosophers. Early in her career she introduced Cassirer to English-speaking readers and has continued to represent a point of view that in many ways is similar to his. Her mature work constitutes one of the most impressive contributions to aesthetics in modern philosophical literature. Among her writings are:

Feeling and Form. New York: Charles Scribner's Sons, 1953.

Philosophical Sketches. New York: Mentor, 1964. See esp. pp. 95-106, 123-52.

Philosophy in a New Key. New York: Mentor, 1951.

(Ed.) *Reflections on Art.* New York: Oxford University Press Galaxy Book, 1961.

Barfield, Owen. *Saving the Appearances: A Study in Idolatry.* London: Faber & Faber, 1957. See esp. p. 157.

Bell, Charles G. "Tragedy," *Diogenes,* No. 7 (Summer, 1954), pp. 12-32.

Bowles, Paul. *Their Heads Are Green and Their Hands Are Blue.* New York: Random House, 1957. See esp. p. 96. Characterizations of his *Time of Friendship* are taken from a review of that book in *Time,* August 4, 1967.

Cross, Farrell. "How to Get More Out of Weekends," *The Reader's Digest* (January, 1968), pp. 125-28.

Gilkey, Langdon. *Shantung Compound.* New York: Harper & Row, 1966. See esp. pp. 96-116.

Glock, Charles Y., and Stark, Rodney. *Christian Beliefs and Anti-Semitism.* New York: Harper & Row, 1966. See esp. pp. 205-7.

Hamilton, Kenneth. "Snake Talk," *The Christian Century*, (March 13, 1968), pp. 326-28.

King, Larry L. "The Cool World of Nelson Rockefeller," *Harper's Magazine* (February, 1968), pp. 31-40.

King, Martin Luther, Jr. *Stride Toward Freedom*. New York: Harper & Row Perennial Library, 1964. See esp. pp. 50-52.

Krikorian, Y. H. "Hocking and the Dilemmas of Modernity," *Philosophy, Religion, and the Coming World Civilization*. Edited by Leroy S. Rouner. The Hague: Martinus Nijhoff, 1966.

Kuhn, Helmut. "Ernst Cassirer's Philosophy of Culture," *The Philosophy of Ernst Cassirer*. Edited by P. A. Schilpp. Evanston: The Library of Living Philosophers, 1949.

Kuzmetsov, Anatoly. *Babi Yar*. New York: Dell, 1967.

MacArthur, A. A. *The Christian Year and Lectionary Reform*. London: SCM Press, 1958.

MacLeish, Archibald. "There Was Something About the Twenties," *Saturday Review* (December 31, 1966), pp. 10-13. A phrase from his *A Continuing Journey* is quoted by Granville Hicks in "Imagination as the End We Seek," *Saturday Review* (January 27, 1968), p. 24.

Morrison, Jim. Characterization of his work is taken from a review in *Time* (November 24, 1967), p. 24.

Napier, B. D. "Prophet," *Interpreter's Dictionary of the Bible*. Edited by G. A. Buttrick. Nashville: Abingdon Press, 1962.

O'Connor, Norman, C.S.P. "New Songs Unto the Lord," *Saturday Review* (April 10, 1965), p. 89.

Schrag, Peter. "Facing the Music," *Saturday Review* (August 19, 1967), p. 61.

Urban, Wilbur M. "The Theological Implications of the Liturgy," *Anglican Theological Review*, XXVIII (1946), 14-27.

West, Jessamyn. *A Matter of Time*. New York: Harcourt, Brace & World, 1966.

White, James F. "Worship in an Age of Immediacy," *The Christian Century* (February 21, 1968), pp. 227-30.

Whitehead, Alfred North. *Adventures of Ideas*. New York: Mentor, 1955. See esp. pp. 169 ff. and 282-95.

Zoll, Donald Atwell. *The Twentieth Century Mind*. Baton Rouge: Louisiana State University Press, 1967. See esp. pp. 140 ff.

A report on the conference on "Myth in Religion and Literature" appears in *The Christian Century* (January 10, 1968), pp. 54, 56.

The experimental translation of the Lord's Prayer was prepared by representatives of three major commissions on worship: the Inter-Lutheran Commission on Worship, the Commission on Worship of the Consultation on Church Union, and the International Committee on English in the Liturgy (Roman Catholic). In making the text available for publication, the spokesman for the three groups stressed the importance of maintaining the line division, capitalization, and punctuation without change.

Index

174